"Jana Kelley does a great job of placing before us the central question that each of us must answer—Will I lay down my fear and claim freedom even when it could cost everything?"

—RUTH RIPKEN and DR. NIK RIPKEN, author of *The Insanity of God* and *The Insanity of Obedience*

"*Door to Freedom* transported me back to a land we once called home. As I read through this novel it brought smiles and tears, reminding me afresh of God's goodness and care for those who dare to serve Him in hard places. Jana captures the culture and the daily challenges for both Muslims and followers of *Isa* (Jesus) living in Sudan, along with the unique challenges facing *khawadjas* (foreigners) living and serving in another culture. *Door to Freedom* is not just a novel but a book containing valuable missions preparation for families that highlights practical issues and emphasizes the call to obey and live courageously—not because of who we are but because of who God is."

—NILANTHI SIM, friend and co-laborer

"Seeking, choosing, and trusting God—no matter the cost—takes on more significance when you live in a country that dictates the limits of both faith and freedom. In her wonderful follow-up novel, *Door to Freedom*, Jana Kelley continues to remind each of us the importance of growing in our faith and confidence in what God has called us to—wherever we live. A call to be bold, brave, and step forward in faith."

—JAMI BELEW, event manager for Women of Faith

"Inspiring, exciting, and moving, Jana Kelley's second novel captures the vibrant culture of North Africa and the ethos of missions to Muslims. *Door to Freedom* realistically portrays the real-life victories and challenges that face missionary families overseas, especially in closed countries. As someone who lived in Sudan with my family for several years, I believe this to be one of the most accurate portrayals of missionary life overseas. The characters are highly developed and the dangerous situations described are very realistic. I highly recommend this book to pastors, church members, and those considering missionary service."

—DR. ROBIN DALE HADAWAY, professor of missions and dean of students at Midwestern Baptist Theological Seminary

"In Jana Kelley's exciting, stand-alone sequel, she weaves a tale of suspense and intrigue. Set in the desert capital of Khartoum, Sudan, Jana provides us with a wealth of cultural insights into the religious traditions adhered to by those mired in their Islamic faith. It is not only insightful but provides a treasure trove of knowledge to those wishing to understand and love their neighbors, both here and abroad, to a saving knowledge of Jesus Christ as Savior and Lord—no matter the cost."

—KATHY HADAWAY, former missionary and adjunct missions professor at Midwestern Baptist Theological Seminary

"I have long known Jana as a gifted writer, and this book further confirmed my suspicions. She is a wonderful storyteller. I could not put *Door to Freedom* down until I had finished it."

—LOIS ROBINETTE, longtime friend, Embrace team leader, and former WMU director at Tabernacle Baptist Church, Ennis, TX

"I was so excited to hear there would be a sequel to *Side by Side*, and it did not disappoint! Jana Kelley's writing draws you into daily life events in Sudan, shows the power of God at work, and brings understanding of a culture very different from our own. I can't wait for the next book!"

—JANA THOMPSON, personal friend

Door to Freedom

A Contemporary Novel

BY JANA KELLEY

NEW HOPE®
PUBLISHERS
Gospel-Centered. Missions-Driven.

Birmingham, Alabama

New Hope® Publishers
PO Box 12065
Birmingham, AL 35202-2065
NewHopePublishers.com
New Hope Publishers is a division of WMU®.

New Hope Publishers serves its authors as they express their views, which may not express the views of the publisher.

Library of Congress Cataloging-in-Publication Data
Names: Kelley, Jana, 1971- author.
Title: Door to freedom : a contemporary novel / by Jana Kelley.
Description: First edition. | Birmingham, AL : New Hope Publishers, [2017]
Identifiers: LCCN 2016040866 (print) | LCCN 2016050193 (ebook) | ISBN
   9781625915160 (softcover) | ISBN 9781596699694 (Ebook)
Subjects: LCSH: Sudan--Social life and customs--Fiction. | Culture
   conflict--Fiction. | Christian life--Fiction. | Muslims--Fiction. | GSAFD:
   Christian fiction.
Classification: LCC PS3611.E4427 D66 2017 (print) | LCC PS3611.E4427
(ebook)
   | DDC 813/.6--dc23
LC record available at https://lccn.loc.gov/2016040866

ISBN-13: 978-1-62591-516-0

N174114 • 0317 • 2.5M1

≳ Dedication ≲

Dedicated to Muslim women who are seeking truth.
May you truly find it.

⇒ Acknowledgments ⇐

Thank you to the Lord, who is worthy of our trust. He opens great doors of opportunity for His children.

Thank you to my husband, Kris, and to my sons Aaron, Seth, and Joel for your enthusiasm, ideas, and unrivaled support for the writing of this book. A big thank you goes to Mom and Dad for always supporting us and encouraging us to "go." Susan and Jenna, you have been my cheerleaders this year, I am so grateful for you. Thank you to my beta readers, you guys were the first to see the manuscript, and I am indebted to you for your encouragement and suggestions. To Natalie Hanemann, you have once again been a huge help to me. Thank you for sharing your expertise. A Texas-sized thanks to all the people at New Hope Publishers for your work in getting this project from idea to published book.

I am filled with gratitude to each of you: whether you are a reader, a prayer supporter, someone who has given me an encouraging word, or someone who has spread the word. Thank you for being part of the group.

⋙ Glossary ⋘

Abaya: robe-like clothing worn by women

Afwan: "You are welcome."

Al baraka feekoom: "Blessing be yours."

Aleykum wassalaam: response to "*Salaam aleykum*"

Alhamdulillah: "Thanks be to God."

Al-hayat: the life

Allah: God

Allahu akbar: "God is the greatest."

Allah ma'ik: "God be with you" or "God go with you."

Allah yabarak feekee: "God bless you."

Amreeka: America

Aseeda: thick, porridge-like food

Astaghfir Allah: "God forgive me."

Bika: Sudanese funeral/ceremony of mourning

Bilakthar: "I miss you more," response to "*mushtagiin.*"

Dilka: homemade scented perfume/body scrub

Dukhaan: smoking incense used in beautification treatments

Eid al-Fitr: festival at the end of Ramadan

Fee ilajla innadaama wa feetaanee issalaama: Arabic proverb translated, "In haste there is regret, but in patience and care there is peace and safety."

Fuloos: coins, spare change

Habeebee (feminine: *habeebtee*)*:* my dear

Haboba: grandmother

Haj: pilgrimage to Mecca that all Muslims should take; title given to one who has taken the pilgrimage

Hibir: ink

Hosh: enclosed outside area of a Sudanese home

Iftaar: breakfast; breaking of the fast during Ramadan

Imam: worship leader of a mosque

Injil: New Testament

Injil Yohana: the Gospel of John

Innoor: the light

Insha' Allah: "if God wills"

Isa: Jesus

Itikaf: Muslim ritual of spending all night (several nights) in a mosque to pray, read the Qur'an, and seek God

Jallabeeya: white robe worn by Northern Sudanese men

Karkaday: hibiscus tea

Khalwa: Islamic school

Khawadja: foreigner or white person

Kitab alMuqaddas: the Holy Bible

Laylat alQadr: the Night of Power

Mabrook: congratulations

Maghribeen: person of Moroccan descent

Malesh: "Don't worry" or "Excuse me."

Masa 'ilxayr: "Good afternoon."

Masa 'innoor: "Light afternoon," response to *"Masa 'ilxayr."*

Masalama: "Good-bye."

Masha' Allah: "Thanks to God."

Masihiiya: Christian

Min zaman ma shuftik: "Long time, no see."

Muezzin: person who calls the faithful to prayer from the mosque, usually broadcast over loudspeakers

Munaqiba: woman who wears a veil over her face in public

Mushtagiin: "I miss you."

Naematan fawq niema: literally "grace upon grace"

Qur'an: the main Islamic holy book

Sabah 'ilxayr: "Good morning."

Sabah 'innoor: "Morning of light," response to *"Sabah 'ilxayr."*

Salaam: peace

Salaam aleykum: Arabic greeting meaning "peace be upon you"

Salaat al-janazah: prayer performed at a Muslim funeral

Salon: seating area for guests

Sambosa: fried meat or vegetable pie

Shawarma: meat wrap

Sheikh: leader at a mosque

Shela: wedding gifts

Shukran: "Thank you."

Souq: open-air market

Subhia: Northern Sudanese bridal dance ceremony

Tabeea: nature

Tageeya: skullcap worn by Northern Sudanese men

Tarha: headscarf worn by Sudanese girls

Ta'meeya: fried snack made from chickpeas

Tobe: colorful full-body scarf worn by married women in Sudan

Utfudulu: used in various situations to mean "welcome" or "help yourself"

Wudhu: ceremonial washing before Muslim prayers

Ya salaam: an exclamation

Youm 'ilqiyaama: the Day of Judgment

Zibeeb: raisin, also the name of a bruise on the forehead caused by bowing forcefully to the ground during prayer

A great door for effective work has opened to me, and there are many who oppose me.

—1 Corinthians 16:9

➳ Chapter 1 ➳

Y ou're a frog in a pot." That's what Mia Weston's mother would say
when she heard the news. "The water is boiling all around you, and
you don't even know it." Maybe she was right.

Mia pondered the thought as she piled the breakfast dishes in the
kitchen sink. For two years she and Michael lived and raised their family in North Sudan. The Islamic country often made news headlines
because of human rights violations and strict adherence to Sharia law.
She couldn't blame her mother for being concerned. But the Sudanese people Mia and her family knew were kind and friendly. Mia and
Michael planned to renew their contract with Kellar Hope Foundation
and stay an additional two years.

Mia imagined the conversation she would have with her mother
over video chat. Mia would explain, once again, how Kellar Hope Foundation was providing food and clothing and better health care and edu-
cation for refugees in Sudan. She would sell the vision for humanitarian
aid organizations like Kellar Hope. And remind her that by legally living
and working in Sudan, they had a unique opportunity to also share the
gospel with their friends and neighbors. Then her mother would remind
her that Sudan was not stable and that the risks outweighed the good
they were doing. The conversation would end with an agreement to dis-
agree, and a sincere but sad, "I love you, Mia." Followed by her own
frustrated, "I love you too, Mom."

That conversation would come later. First, she and Michael would go
to dinner to celebrate their decision to stay. He had already dropped off
nine-year-old Corey and six-year-old Annie at school and headed to the
foundation's office to sign the contract papers. Beth, Mia's best friend,
agreed to babysit Corey, Annie, and four-year-old Dylan. And to think
that Michael had cleared his schedule and arranged it all himself. He
could be so romantic sometimes.

Mia sighed as she surveyed the sink brimming with dirty dishes. All her
friends back home had dishwashers. Mia, however, would be spending
the next hour scrubbing syrup off of plates and wiping sweat from her

brow. Despite the lack of modern conveniences, Mia and her family loved living in Sudan. Even when they hated it. It was wonderful and terrible all mixed into one giant ball of confusion.

Could she ever go back to live in Texas again? Sudan had changed her. She had learned about people in other countries, about herself, and about God. She knew He wanted them here to demonstrate His love to the Sudanese around them. And she knew it was not because she was anything special but because He was faithful.

Mia soaped up a sponge and poured a kettle of warm water into the sink. Her thoughts drifted to Halimah. The fact that the once-Muslim girl had given her heart to Jesus made it impossible for Halimah to remain living at home. The last email Mia received from her indicated that she was in Kenya but gave no details.

Mia shuddered as she remembered what Halimah looked like when she showed up at the Westons' house that fateful day almost a year ago. Her face was swollen and her body tender from the beatings she had received at the hands of her father and brother. If she hadn't found safety in the Weston home, Mia didn't know what would have become of the brave Arab girl. After months of hiding, Halimah's underground church helped her escape the city and finally the country. Now she lived under a new name, Sara. But Mia would always think of her as Halimah.

Few people in Khartoum—the capital city of Sudan—knew that Halimah had lived with the Westons for seven months. Since Michael and Mia did not know Halimah's current whereabouts, they had no information to give, should an angry family member or a policeman question them. But no one had. God had never lifted His hand of protection from them. He was faithful. He was always faithful.

Mia's thoughts were interrupted by her cell phone ringing.

"Hi, babe," Michael spoke in a serious tone. "I'm going to have to stay late at the office today. I think dinner is off the table."

"Why? What do you mean?" Mia fought back a wave of frustration. Michael had been so diligent lately about putting family before work.

"It's Kellar Hope." Michael lowered his voice, even though hardly anyone in the office spoke English. "It's in some kind of trouble. I don't know what it is exactly. That's what I need to stay and find out. It looks like the foundation may have to close. If that's the case we can't stay in Sudan. There'd be no contract to sign."

"Oh. Wow." Mia didn't know what to say. If they couldn't stay in Sudan, they couldn't do what she was sure God wanted them to do. "Well, of course. I understand. Stay as long as you need to." This was a good time for Mia to extend some grace.

"I hope this will blow over and we'll be having our dinner date in a few days."

"Me too." Mia was proud of herself for being so calm.

"Oh, and of course Beth can't come babysit because she's up at the office too."

"Yeah, of course. I understand." Mia sounded more empathetic than she felt. So much for a whole evening of adult conversation with a handsome date. She'd be spending the evening entertaining the kids while her mind played out all the possible scenarios if Kellar Hope Foundation closed and they had to leave Sudan.

***

Michael returned home after Mia had put the kids to bed. She was sitting on the couch, flipping through a two-year-old copy of *Taste of Home*. The only magazines sold in Khartoum were in Arabic, except for the occasional *TIME* magazine that cost five times as much as the cover price. Mia saved all the magazines she brought when they had first moved to Khartoum. She had long since memorized every article and picture, so flipping through this particular copy was only an exercise to alleviate the worry that was tying a knot in her stomach.

Michael's shoulders slumped as he walked in and set his briefcase on the floor. He kissed Mia on the head before sitting down next to her.

"So? What's wrong at Kellar Hope?"

"It's not just Kellar Hope. It's all the small aid organizations that are operating out of Khartoum. The government is making noise like they want them all gone."

"Well, they can't do that. Won't that make the Sudanese government look bad on an international level?"

Michael leaned back and folded his arms behind his head, trying to stretch the stress out of his muscles.

"It's complicated. What they really want is our office and our vehicles. If the government can prove we are doing something wrong, they can confiscate our computers, all of our office equipment, plus all the vehicles."

"Are we doing anything wrong?"

"Not that I know of, but it doesn't really matter. They can make up whatever they want. And there are a lot of Sudanese who work in the office. The government could bribe one of them to keep an eye on us and report anything that could be considered a violation of contract. I heard that one in three men in Khartoum is paid by the secret police to spy on people."

"Is that true?"

"Who knows? But don't worry about it."

"So what do we do?" Mia sat up, stiff-backed on the couch, feeling more and more helpless with each word Michael spoke.

"We can go to bed. I'm exhausted." Michael stood and walked toward the bedroom.

"I'm going to check on the kids first." Mia's tone didn't sound as calm as she wanted it to. But how could Michael expect her not to worry?

After checking on the kids, Mia found Michael lying in bed, eyes shut tight. His breathing was slow and steady. Mia flipped off the light, slipped under the sheets, and closed her eyes.

Questions flooded her mind. What if police raided the office? Would they arrest the workers? Surely they wouldn't bother the Americans. She thought about Hanaan, her Muslim neighbor. Mia had been trying to convince her of Jesus' love and forgiveness. If Mia left, would Hanaan ever believe?

She glanced at the clock on her nightstand. It was midnight. Mia subtracted eight hours in her head: four o'clock in the afternoon in Texas. Her mother would be sitting on the back porch with a glass of iced tea like she did every afternoon. Mia wouldn't tell her about Michael's recent news. His flippant attitude had left her feeling lonely and needing to hear a loving voice. Mom was always good for that.

Mia slipped out from under the covers and tiptoed to the living room. She opened the video chat on the desktop and called her mother. No answer. Strange.

Mia grabbed the house phone from beside the computer and dialed her mother's cell phone number. Michael didn't like it when she used the phone to call home because it was so expensive. This time she didn't care. The phone rang several times and then beeped to record a message.

"Mom, this is Mia. Where are you? Call me."

⇒ Chapter 2 ⇐

Kellar Hope was in trouble. Michael said they should just keep living as if they were going to stay in Sudan. He told Mia so just before heading out the door to take the two older kids to school and then head to work. Mia had forced her head to nod and her voice to say, "Whatever you think is best," but she was still agitated with him for being so calm about everything. She hadn't told him about trying to call her mother. He would say she was just trying to find things to worry about. Somebody had to worry. *Certainly he wasn't.*

If he wanted her to live like she was staying in Sudan, then she was going to hire a maid. Dust, wrinkled clothes, and dirty dishes won out over her desire to do things like she'd always done back home in Texas. Beth, so adept at living in a difficult place like Sudan, had assured her there was no reason for Mia to wear herself out trying to keep the house clean. "Besides," she said to Mia multiple times, "if you hire someone to help you, you are helping them out by giving them a salary."

Perhaps hiring someone to work in her home would distract her from the stress of the storm brewing at the Kellar Hope office and the nagging uneasiness about her mother—who still had not returned her call.

Midmorning, Mia sat across the table from her prospective maid and offered a slight smile. The young woman, a refugee from Eritrea, desperately needed work. Sudan offered her relief from the problems in her own country, but the cost was her home and dignity. Mia considered the small salary she would be offering.

"I need help with sweeping and mopping every day, along with washing and ironing clothes. I also need help washing dishes." As she spoke, Mia glanced down at the white skin of her arm as it glistened with perspiration. She looked across at the woman's smooth chocolate arms resting gracefully on the table. Neither Mia nor this woman belonged in Sudan. One was here by choice, the other by a cruel twist of political fate. Mia coughed, trying to break free from her thoughts. "Your name is Tzega, right? Are you married?"

"Yes. My husband is Ethiopian, and I am Eritrean. Our countries fight, so it is illegal to return to our homes. So, we are here in Sudan . . ."

Mia scribbled an amount on a piece of paper and slid it across the table. "This is what I can pay you every week."

Tzega stared at the paper. Mia tried to decipher her expression. Was the amount enough? Was it lower than the woman expected? Mia had asked Hanaan, her next-door neighbor, what a good salary was and decided on a figure she thought was fair. Now she wasn't so sure.

What would Mia's friends back home say? Having a maid seemed frivolous. But in a desert town like Khartoum, laundry and floor cleaning was a full-time job. A maid in the home could help free up some time for Mia. She determined that she would be willing to pay even a bit more, but just as she opened her mouth to offer it, Tzega looked up and nodded, though her expression remained unreadable.

"It's not enough," she said flatly, "but I have small children, and I need the work. I can start on Monday."

Mia smiled with a calm exterior, but inside, a party broke loose. She would not be left alone to fight the dust and dirt after all. Tzega drank the cup of water that Mia placed in front of her when she had arrived. A cup of water: the customary offering for any guest who walked in from the sweltering sun. Tzega smiled, pulled her scarf back over her head, and shook Mia's hand. Mia saw Tzega to the outer gate and watched her head down the dirt road toward a nearby bus stop, each step wafting puffs of dust and sand into the air behind her.

Mia glanced at her watch. It was the middle of the night in Texas. This was a terrible time to call her mother, but she couldn't wonder any longer. She had to know that everything was OK.

Mia walked back in the house and headed straight for the phone.

"Hello?" Mia's heart flooded with relief when she heard her mother's sleepy voice.

"Mom, it's Mia. Are you OK? Why haven't you returned my calls?"

"It's three in the morning—"

"Well, I . . . yes, I know, but I've been so worried since I hadn't heard from you."

"Mia, your dad is in the hospital. He had a stroke."

The next morning was Friday, a day off in Sudan. Since Northern Sudan was 97 percent Muslim, offices and schools closed on Fridays, and most Sudanese spent the day with their families, the men heading to the mosque for the noon sermon and prayers. Mia was hoping to sleep in. She had not slept well, instead spending most of the night playing out scenarios in her head. Her mother assured her the doctors said the stroke was mild and her dad would fully recover. Mia cried and told her mother that she would come home immediately.

"Mia," she said, "the Lord has called you and Michael to be in Sudan. He is taking care of you, and He is also taking care of us. Don't come home. We'll be fine."

No mention of being a frog in a pot. No mention of missing out on her grandchildren's lives. Mia had been surprised by her mother's strength. And it made her want to go home even more.

At six in the morning Mia heard a ruckus in the kitchen. Groaning, she rolled out of bed. Her head throbbed and her eyes felt swollen. She cried—for a long time—last night when she told Michael about her father. What on earth were the kids doing this early in the morning? When Mia entered the kitchen, she saw Annie and Dylan arranging coffee cups on a tray.

"Good morning, Mommy." Dylan smiled brightly. He held a coffee mug in each hand. Mia noticed one of the mugs was Michael's favorite. She lunged across the room and grabbed the mug out of Dylan's hand, placing it safely on the kitchen cabinet.

"Good morning," she said in as happy a voice as she could muster. "Wow. Why so many mugs?"

Annie smiled. "We didn't know which one you like the best, so we decided to pour coffee in all the mugs and let you choose your favorite."

Mia eyed the coffee machine. Sure enough, coffee was gurgling into the carafe. They must have known she always prepared the coffee machine the night before so in the morning all she had to do was turn it on. At least they hadn't poured the coffee yet—that could have been a disaster. Dylan was infamous for making messes and, even at six years old, Annie could never have managed to carry a tray with eight mugs full of coffee.

"Well, I think I'll use *this* mug." Mia took a blue-and-white mug that said, "I Love Mommy."

"OK," said Dylan, "And I'll pour coffee into the rest of them for Daddy."

Lunging between Dylan and the coffee pot, Mia said, "Oh, that's so nice Dylan, but Daddy is still sleeping. We'll just let him choose his coffee mug when he wakes up. How about you guys eat your breakfast? There are some banana muffins in a container on the counter. Why don't you bring those to the table?"

Dylan busied himself carrying the large plastic container while Mia congratulated herself on another mess diverted. She poured her coffee and stirred in a heaping spoonful of creamer. The thermometer in the window registered 88 degrees. Not bad for Sudan. By ten in the morning, she knew it would read closer to 100. Even in the heat, Mia enjoyed her coffee. A morning cup of coffee forced her to stop, drink slowly, and gather her thoughts for the day ahead. During her morning coffee, she could pray, read Scripture, and listen to the Holy Spirit.

Despite her wish to crawl back in bed and ignore the fact that her dad was in the hospital, Mia joined her three children at the dining table. By this time, Corey, the gentle leader of the bunch, made an appearance. Wiping sleep from his eyes, he quickly fell in step with the other two. Mia watched as he patiently helped Dylan peel the paper liner from the banana muffin.

Mia's heart brimmed with pride. He was so brave two years ago when they moved to Sudan. Instead of attending first grade in one of the best elementary schools in Dallas, Corey now attended a small private school in Khartoum. Though there were a few of other white-skinned foreigners at the school, Corey was in the minority. He'd taken it all in stride. In fact, his best friend was Hanaan's son, little Saleh, who didn't even speak English.

Annie, on the other hand, had cried when she couldn't visit Granny on weekends, but she'd become very adept at operating the computer so that she could talk to her every week. Annie garnered a lot of attention when she was outside of the house—her blond curls and blue eyes attributes very few Sudanese had ever seen except on television.

Then there was Dylan. His face was covered in gooey muffin crumbs, even as his little hand reached into the plastic container for a second helping. Dylan was her challenge. He was into everything. "It's the sign of a healthy, curious boy," her mother told her. Was it wrong to wish he were just a little less healthy and curious?

All in all her family had adjusted well to life in Sudan. Mia had actually been looking forward to extending their time. Now she didn't know what to think.

"Good morning, everyone." Michael interrupted her thoughts with his sleepy greeting as he emerged from the master bedroom.

"Daddy." Dylan waved a crumb-caked hand.

"I made you coffee, Daddy." Annie jumped out of her chair and ran to the kitchen to fetch a mug.

"Hi, Dad." Corey grinned from his place at the table.

Mia smiled at her husband. A day at home with the family. In the past, "family" would have included Halimah. Mia still missed her. But she was in a safe place now, and Mia knew that was best.

Michael rescued the wobbling cup of coffee out of Annie's hands and joined the family at the table.

"After breakfast, how about I fill up the splash pool, and you kids can play outside? Mom and I will watch from the porch."

Mia smiled. The disappointment of the canceled date and Michael's flippant attitude faded. He was really trying to be present with his family when he wasn't at work. He had come a long way in the past two years. Not long ago Mia battled constant frustration toward Michael for all his time at the office. Now it seemed like he really enjoyed spending time with Mia and the kids. *What if we don't get to stay here? We are finally getting the hang of life in this place.*

❧ Chapter 3 ❧

Teacups clinked against each other as Rania carried the tray into the salon, the living room, where her father and three men chatted.

"*Salaam aleykum*," she said quietly as she placed the tray on the coffee table.

Rania's father stopped in midsentence and smiled at his daughter.

"This is my only daughter, my Rania."

"*Aleykum wassalaam*, Rania," said one of the men, responding both to Rania's greeting as well as her father's introduction.

Rania forced a polite smile and busied herself spooning heaps of sugar into the cups and pouring steaming tea. *Why does Father insist on calling me his only daughter? Everyone knows it's a lie. Why do we all pretend?*

Halimah had been gone for a year now, but Rania thought of her every day. Father may have disowned her, but Rania could never do that. Halimah would always be her big sister, even if her name was never spoken in the family.

Rania stirred spoons of powdered milk into the steaming sweet tea and then carefully placed a cup on the table in front of each of the men. When she completed the task, her father grinned proudly, just like he used to do when Halimah served tea to his guests.

"*Utfudulu*," he said, encouraging his guests to help themselves to the tea and a plate piled with cookies and dates.

Rania smiled and quickly extracted herself from the room. She didn't want to be present when her father launched into the merits of marrying his daughter. She was only 16 and had no interest in being married any time soon.

Her father, however, had recently become earnest in his search for her husband. He had already sent messages to her first cousins, asking if any of them were interested in marrying Rania. Even though this was the custom of Sudanese Arabs, Rania hoped it was just a formality. She hoped her cousins would refuse and that her father would find a match for her elsewhere.

Rania returned to the kitchen where her mother stood over a gas burner, stirring a large pot of porridge called *aseeda*.

"I don't know who those men are, Mama, but I don't want to marry any of them. I also don't want to marry a cousin,"

"Rania," Mama said in her comforting voice, "you know it's a good thing to marry your cousin. We know the family. We know that any of your cousins would be an honorable mate and will treat you well. If you marry outside the family, that is a lot of work for your father and me. We have to make sure he comes from an honorable family."

Honor. Honor. It is always about honor. Rania's family was an honorable family, but that was only because her father got rid of the dishonorable one. It was for honor that Rania was called the only daughter. It was for honor that Father tried to beat an evil spirit out of Halimah. And when Halimah left—that mysterious day when she walked out of the house and didn't return—it was for honor that her name was forever banned from their home.

"There are plenty of honorable families besides ours."

"I know there are, dear. Trust your father, he loves you." Mama did not lift her eyes from the pot, but continued to stir the thick liquid.

"Mama," Rania's voice trembled a little. She was afraid to ask the question because she was afraid of the answer. "Do you think Father will let me go to college?"

On rare occasions, Mama let her guard down and spoke honestly with Rania. She stopped stirring but didn't turn around. Her voice was compassionate but steady.

"I don't know, Rania."

"It's not fair." Rania sighed. She didn't wait for her mother to reply. Instead she went to her room and shut the door.

In the past, she was greeted by her sister, Halimah, but now she was greeted by silence. Halimah's bed was still there, but her presence was long gone. Sometimes Mama slept in the bed so Rania would not be alone. If Haboba, Rania's grandmother, came for a visit, she would sleep there. But mostly Rania slept alone. And she hated it.

Why did Halimah leave? Every night for a year, as Rania lay in bed trying to fall asleep without her sister, she asked the same question. Every night she heard her sister's words to her, "Read the book, Rania. It's the most important thing you'll ever read."

Rania obeyed Halimah's instructions—partially anyway. She retrieved the small book from under the mattress where Halimah hid it. But Rania was terrified of the little tome. It was because of books that Father and her older brother Abdu beat Halimah that fateful night. Rania was not as brave as Halimah. She refused to be caught with a dangerous book.

On the other hand, what if the book really did contain the answer Rania was looking for? What if the book explained why Halimah disappeared? Rania hadn't known what to do. So she wrapped the book in a dishcloth and stuffed it in the bottom of an old purse. Then she hid the purse behind her wardrobe. She was afraid to throw it away, but she was afraid to look inside it.

Rania thought about that book every day. But she never retrieved it. Instead, when she was troubled, she would take out an art book and her colored pencils, and she would draw. This day was no different.

One day, I will learn to paint. She settled on her bed, leaning against the wall with her legs propping her art book like an easel. She sketched the outline of a tree. *It's ugly, Rania. It looks like a little kid drew it.* She threw her pencils on the floor in frustration. Leaning her head against the wall and closing her eyes, she thought about the book again. Maybe it was time to look at it.

⇒ Chapter 4 ⇐

Rania stared at her wardrobe. There was a small gap between the large wooden piece of furniture and the wall. No one would notice the arrangement except Rania. She'd been careful to place the old purse upright against the wall so that it created as narrow an obstacle as possible before she leaned her back against the wardrobe and shoved it against the wall. There it remained for the better part of a year. She never mentioned the book, just as she never mentioned Halimah.

Today was different. Rania took a deep breath and tiptoed across her bedroom to the door. As quietly as she could, she twisted the skeleton key to lock the door. If anyone came, she'd just say she was changing clothes and had locked the door since there were guests in the salon.

She placed both of her hands on the back corner of the wardrobe, near her bed, and wrapped her fingers around the sharp edge. She pulled as hard as she could. The solid wood wardrobe creaked as it moved forward about an inch. It was enough. Rania reached one hand behind the wardrobe as far as she could. Cobwebs tangled in her fingers, but she felt the fake-leather purse and grabbed it. It was filthy, and Rania brushed it off before crawling back on her bed to inspect its contents.

She pulled the dishcloth out of the purse and felt the weight and shape of the book. Could such a small object really solve the mystery of Halimah? She carefully unfolded the cloth and stared. The book was thin with a blue paper cover. Yellow letters on the front read *Injil Yohana*.

The pages were filled with printed words. She flipped through the book from beginning to end. Disappointment settled in Rania's chest. She had half expected to find a piece of paper with a note from Halimah. Her big sister had promised that this book contained answers for her disappearance. But in fact, there was nothing inside the book. Only printed words.

Rania set the book down on the bed next to her sketchpad. She glanced at the tree she'd drawn. Sure, it was elementary looking. But she was just learning. She'd get better.

She was about to stuff the book back into its dusty tomb when she heard laughter coming from the salon. She rolled her eyes. Her father must have taken out the alcohol for his friends. The men visiting her father only got that loud when they were tipsy. And that only happened on occasion, when, late at night, her father would pull out the illegal drinks he kept hidden in his room.

There had to be an answer in the book. Halimah had been adamant. Rania was tired of pretending. She pretended her father didn't drink. She pretended she didn't have a big sister. She pretended she wanted to get married rather than go to school. Surely there was a better way. Maybe the book would have more than one answer.

She picked it up again and flipped to the first page.

"In the beginning was the Word, and the Word was with God, and the Word was God. He was with God in the beginning." The words flowed poetically, and Rania found herself mesmerized by their rhythm. The words were beautiful like the Qur'an. But this book wasn't an Islamic one.

"Through him all things were made; without him nothing was made that has been made. In him was life, and that life was the light of all mankind. The light shines in the darkness, and the darkness has not overcome it."

Life and light. I could use a little of both.

≫ Chapter 5 ≪

The kids splashed and danced in the plastic pool that Michael filled with water from the garden hose. Mia and Michael settled on the veranda to finish the last of the coffee.

"So I was thinking," Michael said. "We should start reading the Bible together."

Mia choked on her coffee, and her eyes began to water as she gulped the steaming liquid. It burned in her throat. She willed a calm response.

"Sure, I think that would be great."

Mia's heart beat in excitement. Michael was a faithful Christian. He insisted they attend church, pray before the meals, and read Bible stories to the children. But he never initiated something like this.

"Maybe we can wake up half an hour earlier each day and read. I was thinking we could start in Acts. You know, that's where Paul goes to share the gospel in foreign countries. We might be able to relate."

Mia recovered from the initial shock and ignored the burning sensation in the back of her throat. *Wake up earlier? I am already exhausted.* But the excitement of studying the Bible with her husband trumped the disappointment of losing sleep.

As the children continued to play, Mia and Michael read the first chapter of Acts together, taking particular note of verse seven when Jesus told His disciples, "It is not for you to know the times or dates the Father has set by his own authority."

"I can't help but think that's for us too," Mia said. "Who knows how this problem at Kellar Hope is going to turn out? We don't know if we will get to stay or have to leave. But I guess that's not really for us to know."

"And then look at the next verse. Jesus says His disciples will receive power, and they will be witnesses for Him. I guess that message is for us too."

"Believe it or not, that's what Mom told me on the phone yesterday. She said that I needed to trust God and that He would give me the courage to stay here and to share Jesus' love with others."

Michael placed his Bible on the table and tented his fingers. He stared at the children, but Mia could tell his thoughts were on the passage. "You know, I've been wondering. Maybe we need to be bolder in our efforts to bring Jesus to our Muslim friends. Sure, we've told our friends that we believe in Jesus. But we haven't really shared the whole gospel, I mean, explained that they can believe in Him too. Maybe we should do that."

Just then, drops of water sprinkled across the two, and Dylan giggled from across the yard. "I got you." The littlest of the three swimmers laughed. He held the water hose and grinned as big as a clown.

"Oh, you did, did you?" Michael countered. He stood to his full six feet and stomped toward Dylan playfully. Dylan screeched and dropped the water hose as he ran. The other kids laughed and ran. Annie ran to Mia as if she was home base, and Corey ran to the abandoned water hose in an attempt to spray his dad.

But Mia was focused on how she could step up her efforts to share the good news with her neighbors.

⁓⁓⁓

Khartoum International Christian Fellowship met on Sunday evenings in a borrowed room at one of the few local church compounds. Mia didn't mind sitting in plastic chairs and being cooled only by ceiling fans. The praise songs lifted her spirits, and the Scripture reading comforted her soul. After a challenging week, the fellowship of other believers at KICF gave her the strength she craved.

She herded her kids toward an empty row of chairs halfway to the front of the room. Beth had saved a place for them.

Beth smiled and gave her a hug. "Sorry I couldn't babysit for you the other night."

"Are you kidding? You have more to worry about than that. How are you handling all the tension at the office?"

Beth was a pillar of faith. She always seemed confident and in control, so Mia was surprised to see her friend's brow wrinkle.

"It's hard actually. Seems to be getting worse. I don't know what's going to happen."

"I'm sure it will all be sorted out soon," Mia said, giving her friend's hand a squeeze. She hoped she sounded reassuring.

The worship leader began the service with a praise song as people continued to file in and find places to sit.

Beth leaned down toward Mia. "How are things with you?"

"Michael and I are reading from the Book of Acts together every day. You know, Jesus' disciples weren't scholars; they were just regular people like us. But they were so bold when they told unbelievers about Jesus. I can't figure out how to do that with Hanaan. I keep hoping she'll want to know more about Jesus, but I don't know . . . I'm running out of new things to talk about with her."

"Why don't you try getting her to teach you something? Maybe you need a project to do together."

"Hmm . . . that's a good idea. I could ask her to teach me to cook something."

Mia and Beth turned their attention back to the music, and Mia closed her eyes. She let the voices around her pour over her and the lyrics feed her soul. After several songs and a Scripture reading, the children were dismissed to Sunday School in a separate room. She watched her own three children make their way down the aisle and join the rest of the children.

The pastor, an Irish man who had lived in Khartoum for several years, preached about perseverance—a fitting subject for all that was going on in Mia's life at the moment. She was thankful for a gathering of believers and a place to worship in English, though most of the people were from European or African countries.

After one of the elders, who was from Kenya, said the closing prayer, Beth turned to Mia. "How's your dad?"

"He's doing better. Mom says he'll be home from the hospital in a few days. I just feel terrible that I can't be there." Mia smiled at her friend, but her heart ached at the question. Was she doing the right thing by staying?

⇒ Chapter 6 ⇐

Mia buried herself in training Tzega how to clean house. Maybe it would get her mind off her dad and all the uncertainty at Keller Hope. She had only been able to send and receive short text messages since her mother was at the hospital all day and too tired to talk at night. But those few messages assured her of her father's improvement. Mom said he was complaining about the hospital food. And he told her to relay a message to Mia—not to worry, he was fine. And, he would be home soon.

Tzega was quiet and had a very agreeable personality, but she had never worked in a home with tile floors and indoor plumbing. Mia found herself teaching Tzega basic cleaning etiquette. For one thing, towels used to dry dishes should not also be used to mop the kitchen floor. Another matter to address: wet laundry needed to be hung on the clothes line, not the rose bushes. Using a mixture of Arabic and English, Mia showed Tzega how to use "the spray bottle with blue liquid" to clean the mirrors and "the spray bottle with white liquid" to clean the shower and toilets. Tzega had never seen so many categories of cleaning rags and disinfectant potions and had never heard so many rules for how to keep a house tidy.

"*Khawadjas*, white foreigners, are kind of particular about these things," Mia admitted. Tzega smiled sweetly and did her best to follow Mia's instructions.

One day, Mia taught Tzega to fry potato chips. She showed her how to cut thin slices with a vegetable peeler and dip them in a pot of hot oil. Mia didn't enjoy this tedious job, but the kids loved the snack, and potato chips were hard to find in stores. Corey and Annie were in school until the afternoon, and the whole process of making potato chips fascinated Dylan. He sat quietly on a kitchen chair and watched Tzega with great interest. Mia took the opportunity to slip out and visit Hanaan next door.

Mia recently bought an *abaya* to wear over her clothes when leaving the house. The long black robe snapped in the front so it was easy to slip on over the capris and short-sleeved T-shirt she wore. Most of the time,

Mia changed into long skirts and long sleeves to leave the house. But since she often made visits next door, she found the *abaya* to be much more convenient. Hanaan, of course, was pleased Mia was adapting so well to Sudanese culture.

"You would make such a good Muslim," Hanaan said on several occasions. Mia was glad to make such a good impression, and her heart told her this was a great transition into a spiritual conversation. But she wasn't sure how to get there, so she just smiled. That's how it was with Hanaan.

A year earlier, Halimah, who was living with Mia at the time, told her Hanaan was very close to accepting Christ. Mia prayed almost daily for Hanaan and tried to mention Jesus every time they visited. She had been so sure that Hanaan would eventually understand that Jesus was the only way to be sure of going to heaven. But days had turned to months. Now it had been a year, and Hanaan didn't seem any more interested in Jesus than the first time Mia had spoken of Him.

After reading Acts with Michael, however, Mia felt bold again. She prayed for an opportunity.

Morning was not the normal visiting time for families, but Sudanese women often visited each other in the mornings once their husbands were at work. Mia rang Hanaan's doorbell and stood on the sidewalk outside the privacy wall around Hanaan's house. She glanced down the dust-covered street. Even though they lived in an upper-class neighborhood, the roads were filled with dirt and broken cement. Somewhere, far under the rubble, were the remains of a tarmac road.

Mia heard footsteps. She recognized the rhythm of Hanaan's gait. It was the shuffle of her tired feet heaving her ample body down the driveway.

"*Salaam aleykum.*" Mia called out the traditional greeting to let Hanaan know who was on the other side.

Hanaan opened the metal gate. "*Aleykum wassalaam.*" Her friend was clad in a bright blue muumuu-style dress with the ever-present headscarf pinned tightly around her plump face.

"I just came to visit a few minutes before I feed Dylan lunch."

"Of course, you are always welcome." Hanaan pointed to a set of metal chairs on the veranda. "Please, sit here."

As Mia sat down, a dark young woman emerged through the front door with a tray and a cup of water.

"Oh, thank you." Mia took the cup from the tray and smiled at the young lady.

"Bring some tea, Didi." Hanaan said to the lady. Her tone was curt.

Didi disappeared and Hanaan turned her attention to Mia.

"You don't have to talk to the workers in my house."

"What do you mean?"

"That girl, Didi. She just works here. You don't have to talk to her like she belongs."

Mia sensed the Holy Spirit nudging her. She felt like a schoolgirl being urged to ask someone to the middle-school dance. Mia forged ahead awkwardly.

"She is a person, just like you and me, and that's how Jesus sees her."

Mia drank her glass of water and set it on the round metal table between them. She looked up and saw that Hanaan was staring at her.

"You always speak so highly of Jesus."

"Because He is wonderful. Did you know that Jesus has power over nature?" *Mia, what on earth does that have to do with Jesus seeing people?*

"What do you mean?"

"Well, one day Jesus was in a boat with His disciples. He was so tired and He fell asleep. Suddenly, a storm came and the disciples were afraid the boat would crash and they would die."

"What did they do?"

"They woke Jesus up and said, 'Don't you care?' Then He got up and spoke to the storm. The wind and waves stopped, and it became calm."

"That's a nice story."

"Jesus cares about us too." Mia's heart raced.

"Your Arabic has gotten very good, Mia."

"Oh, thank you. But what do you think about the story—do you think Jesus has power over nature?"

"You are using the wrong word for 'nature,' Mia. You should say 'tabeea.'"

"Umm, thank you. What do you think about the story?"

"Ah, Didi has arrived with the tea. Put it here, Didi. Did you bring sugar? Oh, yes, here it is. Put three spoons of sugar in each cup. No, do the sugar first. Don't you know that? Put the sugar in, and then you can pour the tea. There, just like that. Did you put cinnamon in the tea? Mia likes cinnamon."

Mia sighed, her enthusiasm doused by a rant on how to make tea properly. Should she ram her will right on through just to ease her own conscience? The gospel was relational. What kind of friend would she be if she crammed the good news down Hanaan's throat? She shifted gears.

"I would love to learn how to cook Sudanese food, but I don't know where to start. Could you help me?"

A smile spread across Hanaan's face. "*Masha' Allah*, you want to learn to make Sudanese food. Of course I can teach you. We'll start with something basic like *aseeda*. Have you had it? It's a delicious porridge and is unique to Sudan. Tomorrow Didi will go to the *souq* and buy the ingredients."

Mia looked up at Didi as the young woman stirred their cups of tea. "Thank you, Didi."

Didi raised her eyebrows in surprise when Mia said her name. She smiled and said, "You are welcome."

Hanaan smirked.

⇒ Chapter 7 ⇐

Mia returned home to the delicious aroma of fried potato chips. What Southern girl is not tempted by fried anything? And homemade potato chips? Well, that beat any packaged snack a potato chip company could dream up. Tzega proved herself adept at handling the job.

"These look wonderful," Mia said as she entered the kitchen. She took a chip off the top of the brimming bowl. "Mmmmm, yes, very nice. Did you try one?"

"No," said Tzega.

"Here, take this." She handed her one. "They are better with a little salt." Mia grabbed the saltshaker off the spice rack and sprinkled the potato chips.

"They are very good," Tzega said taking a tentative bite and then popping the rest of the chip in her mouth.

Tzega was not a talkative person, but Mia was thankful that she spoke Arabic and a little English. Since Tzega was Eritrean, her mother tongue was Tigrinya. Mia knew nothing about Tigrinya except that it had a funny looking script and the pronunciation was much different. Arabic was difficult enough.

Tzega turned her attention to washing dishes while Mia made peanut butter-and-jelly sandwiches. Dylan, who had ventured off to his room and become interested in a basket of building blocks, would be asking for lunch soon.

"Do you know how to cook *aseeda*?"

"No," Tzega said.

Mia noticed that she had paused before responding. "Do you not like it? My neighbor says it is very good."

Tzega grabbed a tea towel and began to dry a plate. "The Sudanese love to eat *aseeda*. But I am not Sudanese."

"My neighbor is going to teach me how to make it."

Tzega wrinkled her nose in distaste. "Maybe you will like it."

"Now I am not so sure," Mia said and laughed.

Mia was exhausted by dinnertime. That was nothing unusual, though she had hoped hiring Tzega would change that. As it turned out, the incessant heat coupled with the amount of work it took to keep the house running was tiring whether one person did it or two. Still, Mia was grateful to have Tzega's help in the mornings. Fatigue was just part of the package deal of living in Khartoum.

She set the table but left the beef stew and bread in the kitchen until Michael arrived. He would be tired, too. He always was. Mia expected that he would also most likely be discouraged with all that was going on at work. She wondered if he had learned any more news about the situation there.

To her surprise, Michael walked in the door with a giant grin.

"Hi, honey. Are things worked out at the office?"

Michael set his briefcase down just inside the front door. "What? The office? Oh, no. The problems at the office are just the same. Probably worse. But I had a chance to talk to Habiib about Jesus."

"Talking about Jesus is good, Daddy." Dylan, fists full of Lego pieces, ran from his room straight toward Michael as if he would crash into his father's legs. Michael grabbed the chubby boy and flung him up onto his shoulders. Dylan squealed. Lego pieces tumbled to the floor.

"You're so happy, Dad." Corey stood in the doorway of the bedroom that the children shared.

Mia wondered if Corey had been noticing the strain on Michael's face whenever he returned from the office.

Michael smiled and tickled Dylan's feet, which were draped over his shoulders. Dylan squealed again and belly laughed, his blond curls bobbled like springs. "I'll tell you all about it at dinner."

"Dinner?" asked Annie, who emerged from behind Corey. "Hi, Daddy."

"Hello, princess."

Mia returned to the kitchen to bring in the stew. She fought to make sense of the scene in the other room. The one with the happy father and the delighted children. She didn't understand how he could be so happy when the office was in such jeopardy. Surely there was good news from the office. Maybe Michael was just waiting until dinner to surprise her.

With the family seated around the table, Michael led them in a prayer of thanksgiving for the food and began to dish the rich stew into bowls.

Mia tried to wait but her curiosity forced the words out of her mouth. "So, tell us about work. Something good happened."

"I told you," Michael said, grinning. "I got to share with Habiib."

"What did you share with him, Daddy?" Dylan asked.

"I shared Jesus."

"Oooooh," Dylan exclaimed. "That's goooooood."

"So what did you say, honey? Give me specifics. I mean, Habiib knows we are Christians."

"Right," said Michael. "I was praying for an opportunity to share more of the teachings of Jesus, and it came." He was virtually floating, his eyes sparkled with excitement. Who was this man? Had applying God's Word really changed him that much? He had always been enthusiastic about sharing the gospel, but now he seemed different, in a good way. "It started very simple, really. Habiib was reading the newspaper, and he found an article on the Five Pillars of Islam. He wanted me to read it."

"What are the five pills, Daddy?" Dylan looked confused.

"Five pillars. They are five things all faithful Muslims do. Praying five times a day is one of them. Fasting for a month each year is another one."

"So they have to do the five things to be good?" Corey asked.

"That's what I asked Habiib. I said, 'Do you have to do these things in order to go to heaven?'"

"What did he say?" Mia asked.

"Well, after he talked about the importance of each of the five things, he said that hopefully Allah would let him into heaven. And then he looked at me and asked me what I thought."

"Is that when you talked about Jesus?" Corey asked.

"Well, I told Habiib that those who believe in Jesus can be sure they will go to heaven because it is not based on their own actions or good deeds."

"I want to tell Saleh about Jesus," Corey said. "I know he's Muslim, but I think he should know about Jesus."

"I think he should too," Michael said.

"I'm going to start praying for him." Corey's voice was resolute.

"Habiib said he'd like us to come talk to him and his wife together," Michael said after the children had excused themselves from the table and wandered off to play.

"That's great. When can we do it?"

"Well, that's the tricky part."

"What do you mean?"

"Well, Habiib said he was interested to talk more, but that we needed to be very careful. He confirmed that there are spies at the office. I could get in trouble for talking about Jesus. That would put Kellar Hope in a bad situation."

"Kellar Hope is already in a bad situation."

"I know. And if I'm caught telling Muslims about Jesus, I could make it worse."

Mia put her spoon down on the table. She didn't feel like eating anymore. "So, what are you going to do?"

"Well," said Michael, "we've been reading in Acts, right? We've been saying we need to do what the men in Acts did. So I shouldn't stop."

"It's one thing, honey, for me to share with Hanaan. Sure, I might risk our friendship, but that's about it. What you are talking about is the possibility of risking your job. Or worse, Habiib's job."

"Habiib doesn't really work for Kellar Hope. He's just a consultant, hired for specific work. I think he was more concerned for me."

"And you aren't?"

"I'm more concerned about the need to share Jesus. Really, Mia, ever since we started reading Acts, I've started seeing the importance of sharing the truth. I think we should trust the results—or maybe the consequences—to God."

⇒ Chapter 8 ⇐

Maysoon was one of the reasons Rania had not fallen into depression after Halimah disappeared. She was no more than an acquaintance before then, but when Rania began to spend her days crying in her bedroom, Mama requested that Maysoon come visit. Maysoon often walked home from school with Rania. The more Maysoon spent time with Rania, the less Rania cried.

The girls spent hours talking and pouring through magazines Maysoon brought to Rania's house. They read the life stories of popular Arab movie stars and drooled over the beautiful sequined clothes and posh houses that filled the glossy pages of the periodicals.

Maysoon was spunky and brave like Halimah. She was also respectful to her parents. Rania liked that. She wanted to be respectful too. She wanted to stop crying, but she missed Halimah so very much. As the weeks after Halimah's departure turned to months, Rania and Maysoon formed a strong bond. Maysoon let Rania talk about her sister, which was a salve to Rania's aching heart.

Maysoon encouraged Rania to draw and planted in her the dream of being a painter one day. With Maysoon's accolades, Rania's desire to become an artist had blossomed into a full-fledged life goal. During one of her normal all-afternoon visits, Maysoon flipped through Rania's sketchbook. Rania bit her lip and watched her friend.

Maysoon was tall and slim. Her hair, if left alone, was kinky. But Maysoon took great care to keep her hair straightened and shiny with a variety of oils and hair products. She kept her long black locks gathered in a loose ponytail and covered with a scarf most of the time, even in the house. But when she sat with Rania in the privacy of her room, she immediately took off her scarf, removed the hair tie and spent the first five minutes of every visit in front of Rania's mirror, fluffing her hair so that it hung gracefully past her shoulders. Rania stifled a reverent jealousy. Her own hair never grew that long, no matter how many kinds of oils she tried. What did it matter? Like every Muslim girl, Rania always covered her hair with a *tarha*.

Unlike Maysoon, Rania didn't actually care much about her own hair. She took pride in her soft smooth skin. It was the color of a latte, much lighter than Halimah's or Maysoon's. Light skin was good enough for her.

"*Masha' Allah.*" Maysoon's voice pierced through Rania's vain thoughts. "Praise Allah. Your drawings are really beautiful. I can't believe you can be this good without formal training. Are you sure you aren't taking some secret lessons from someone? Maybe some good-looking guy from across town?" Maysoon's eyes sparkled.

Rania laughed. "Yeah, right. Like you ever see me leave my house for anything but school or going to the market with Mama." Rania eyed her artwork skeptically over Maysoon's shoulders. "I would love to have formal training. I'm hoping Father won't marry me off before college."

"Do you think he'll actually let you go to college? I thought he said that letting Halimah go to college was the fatal mistake."

"He only said that once. That was a long time ago . . ." Her father had said those words the day Halimah disappeared. Not once had she heard the name of her sweet sister come from her father's lips since then. In his next breath he declared that Rania was his one and only daughter: as if he could just pronounce the words and they would become truth for the whole family. A tear trembled on Rania's eyelid.

"I'm sorry," Maysoon said. "I didn't mean to remind you."

"It's OK." Rania grabbed the sketchbook out of Maysoon's hands in an attempt to shake off the sadness. "Here, I want to show you this." She flipped to one of the last pages and held it up for Maysoon to see.

On a background of black, swirls of green and blue at the top of the page flowed into oranges, reds, and yellows in the middle of the page. Toward the bottom, in colors that resembled the climax of a sunset, were two words in elegant calligraphy. *Innoor* and *Al-hayat* swirled around each other so that Maysoon had to look closely to read them.

"*Ya salaam*, Rania, that's beautiful, why does it say 'the light' and 'the life'? Are you talking about nature, or are you talking about your dreams, or what?"

"A little of both, I guess." Rania inadvertently looked toward the wardrobe. She wasn't ready to tell Maysoon about the book yet. But she couldn't shake the words from her mind. Different from her earlier drawings where she unleashed her sadness, her recent drawings seemed to reflect another tone—maybe it was hope. Would she bring some sort of curse on her recent happiness if she told Maysoon about the book? She'd better not risk it just yet.

"Well, it's gorgeous, *habeebtee*, my dear. You are going to be a true artist someday. You've got talent."

"What good is talent if Father won't let me go to college?"

"Well . . ." Maysoon's eyes twinkled. "I do have one idea."

"What's that?"

"You could bring your artwork to the Jadeed Cultural Center."

"Where is that, and how do you know about it? I've never heard you talk about it."

Maysoon grinned. "That's because I never told you about it. But I think it's time you know." She pulled a magazine out of her school bag. This one looked very different from the glossy *Arab Woman* magazines. It was cheap looking and tattered, as if it had been flipped through count-less times. The front cover boasted what Rania guessed was some sort of hip-hop group.

"What is this?" Rania's curiosity got the best of her as she reached for the magazine.

"It's my secret," Maysoon said, looking reverently at the cover picture that was now in Rania's hands. "I want to be a hip-hop star."

Rania looked at her friend in disbelief. Should she let out the laugh that danced in her throat right now? She faked a cough instead.

Maysoon read her surprise anyway, and her brow furrowed. "Hey, I'm always telling you to go after your dream to be an artist. Hip-hop is an art too. What if I want to sing hip-hop? Can't I have my own dream?"

Maysoon was right, of course. She had spent many months cheering up Rania and encouraging her to have her own identity and pursue art. Why shouldn't her best friend have a dream too?

"OK," Rania said, "Hip-hop. I've never heard you sing anything but Sudanese music. Sing me a hip-hop song."

"Not right now. Your parents will hear. What part of the word *secret* did you not get?" Maysoon laughed. "You'll have to come to the JCC to hear me."

"The what?"

"Rania, don't be so dense, the Jadeed Cultural Center. They are hosting an art expo soon and I think I might get to be part of a hip-hop group that will perform. Will you come?"

"You know I don't like to trick Father and Mama, and they will never let me go to something like that."

Maysoon's brow wrinkled again. How could Rania say no to her best friend? She lay the strange magazine on her lap and grabbed her friend's hand, "Of course I'll figure out a way to come."

"Great, I'll let you know when the expo is. I'm going to the JCC tonight, and I'll find out more."

"Your father lets you?"

"Are you kidding? No way, I'm telling him that I'm with you. Wait." Maysoon grabbed Rania's arm. "You aren't going anywhere are you?"

"Me? Ha, no. Do I ever? I'll be here. Do I have to lie for you?"

"No, Father trusts me, he won't come to check."

How did she do it? How did Halimah do it? How did daughters lie to their fathers? Rania just couldn't. It wasn't because she was a good person. She was often tempted to lie. The real reason she didn't was fear. She was terrified. What if she were beaten or banished from the family? She knew she wasn't strong enough to bear such a thing. Rania was no Halimah and she was no Maysoon. Rania would stay home and obey Father until he found a man for her to marry. Surely Allah would reward her obedience. Didn't it count for something?

A strong rap on the door startled both girls, and Rania flung the hip-hop magazine under her bed just as the door opened. Mama's full figure filled the entrance. She eyed the sketchbook that sat on the bed between the two girls and Rania was immediately grateful that her reflexes had caused her to hide the magazine. The older woman smiled at the girls.

"*Salaam aleykum*, Maysoon. Your father called for you. He said your cell phone must be turned off, and he wants to you to come home."

Maysoon opened her purse and dug for her phone. She retrieved it and pressed a button. "*Ya salaam*, the battery is dead. Sorry about that, Um Abdu." Maysoon addressed the woman "Mother of Abdu" as everyone in the neighborhood did. "I'll go home right away."

Mama smiled at Maysoon. Mama would never be upset with the girl who had saved Rania from depression. "*Malesh*, Maysoon, don't worry. I'm sure your father will understand." The older woman turned to leave the room but abruptly whirled back around, Rania thought at first she might fall over at the sudden change of direction. "Oh, girls," she exclaimed, "did you hear about Amal? She's going to get married to Haj Azeez. *Alhamdulillah*. Praise Allah." Before the girls could react, she twirled back around and closed the door behind her.

The teen girls looked at each other in disbelief. Amal to marry Haj Azeez?

"*Ya salaam*," Rania muttered.

"Amal is our age."

"And Haj Azeez is older than Father."

"He already has children, why does he want a second wife? Stop, don't answer that. I don't want to know. Poor Amal."

"Do you think her father will listen to her if she objects?"

"Amal's father? Nope. He's even stricter than my father. I'd say it's a done deal for her. She might as well start making room for wedding gifts."

Rania hated to gossip about a fellow classmate, but it wasn't gossip if she was just talking to her best friend, right? "I heard that Amal has a boyfriend."

"Everyone knows that, Rania. Maybe even her parents. But there's no way they would let her marry Adam. He's not Arab. He's from Darfur."

Rania didn't get into politics that much, but she knew that the Arab government in Khartoum did not look highly on the people of Darfur. They were of African descent, not Arab. And even though they were Muslims, blood apparently ran deeper than religion. No

Arab who wanted to keep their family line pure would marry someone from Darfur.

"Maybe Amal agreed to the decision."

Maysoon snorted as she fished the tattered magazine out from under Rania's bed and stuffed it in her oversized purse. She obviously did not believe those words to be true.

"I gotta go. See you tomorrow morning?"

"Yes, see you then. Maybe we can go by Amal's and walk with her to school tomorrow."

"That's a sweet thought, Rania. But I don't want to get too friendly with Amal. Father may decide that marrying an old man is a good idea for me too." She looked at Rania and a twinkle returned to her eyes. "That won't help me develop my hip-hop image."

She smiled and patted Rania on the leg before stopping by the mirror to tie back her hair and cover the black locks with a floral printed *tarha*. Throwing her bag over her shoulder and heading out the door, she waved good-bye. Rania didn't bother to walk her friend to the outside gate. Maysoon was like family. Instead, she sat on her bed and looked down at her sketchbook. If Maysoon could be a hip-hop star, why shouldn't she pursue art? Hope crept into her heart.

Hope. That's what Amal's name meant. Rania's face clouded. Hope slipped out of her heart and, as if following Maysoon, slipped out the bedroom door.

⇒ Chapter 9 ⇐

Rania searched through the blouses hanging in her wardrobe. *There's nothing in here I want to wear.* It was Friday afternoon, and Rania bet Jamal would be coming for a visit. Father had taken to inviting Halimah's old college buddy, along with several other men, to watch soccer on his large television whenever his favorite team was playing. *Jamal probably wants to go watch the game in the stadium live, but he'll not say no to Father.*

Tonight *Al-Merreikh* was playing their big rival, *Hilal.* Both were Khartoum teams, and the city was evenly divided as far as loyalty to the teams. *Al-Merreikh* was Father's favorite, and she knew he'd be watching. Rania had a hunch that Father had his eye on Jamal, but the reason why still eluded her. Was Jamal a legitimate suitor for Rania, or was Father trying to get information about Halimah's whereabouts?

Rania shuddered as she remembered a conversation between her parents several months ago. Halimah's name was not mentioned, of course, since her father forbade that.

"We should contact her and tell her we forgive her," Mama pleaded. Rania heard the voices in the kitchen late one night, when everyone should have been asleep. "We should invite her to come home."

"The only thing that will bring honor back to our family name is her blood." Father's words were deep and angry. For a moment, Rania held her breath, waiting to hear the slap of her father's palm across Mama's face.

Rania's heart tightened in her chest as she thought about that night and the one thing she feared more than a slap from her father. Halimah once told Rania that Father had said, "I divorce you," to Mama twice. According to Islam, if he said it one more time, it would become reality. It wasn't that Father wanted to divorce Mama, it was just that he had such a quick temper. Most of the time, Mama had good conversations with Father. But every once in a while, he would lose his temper. He certainly did that night, and Rania feared he would pronounce a divorce. But he didn't. Mama took good care of him and had given him four children. Perhaps he remembered how good he had it.

Why did Halimah have to leave? Why can't Father consider letting her come home? But even if he did, would she be safe?

Rania eyed the clothes in her closet again. If Halimah were still at home, she'd ask to borrow one of her outfits. She always had better clothes anyway. Rania used to whine and nag Halimah to lend her clothes. Usually Halimah would yell at her and refuse, but toward the end, she changed. Halimah became gracious and kind toward Rania. What had made her that way? Did the book hidden behind the wardrobe have the answers?

Rania quickly selected a solid navy blouse and a long floral skirt from the closet. Should she wear jewelry? Was that too much, just to be serving tea to Father and his guests?

She pulled a small black box down from the top shelf above the hanging rack. Rania was only sixteen, and even though Father could afford it, she didn't own much gold jewelry. That would come later, from her future fiancé. For now, she had three sets of earrings. One set of dangle earrings was not actually hers. They had been Halimah's.

Rania remembered the day Halimah let her choose a set of earrings to wear. Rania had chosen the nicer pair, and Halimah had worn a smaller, simpler set. *Gracious and kind. Why?*

Rania ran her fingers over the gold filigree. These earrings were the only possession of Halimah's that had not been confiscated and destroyed by her parents when Halimah confessed to believing in Jesus instead of Mohammed. Because Rania had borrowed them, they were not in Halimah's jewelry box that fateful night.

She slipped the earrings through the piercings in her ears and replaced her housedress with the blouse and skirt. Before serving tea to her father and his guests, she'd add a matching scarf to cover her hair.

The soccer game wouldn't start for another hour or so. Rania fished the purse out from behind its hiding place and pulled out the small book, carefully unwrapping the dishcloth.

The words mesmerized her as she reread the first chapter.

"Out of his fullness we have all received grace in place of grace already given."

Naematan fawq niema. Grace in place of grace already given? What could that mean? Halimah was gone. How could that be a grace?

She kept reading. She read about a man named *Andrawoos* who told his brother *Butrus* about *Isa*, Jesus. That's what Halimah had done for her, right? She had pointed her to this book that taught her about grace and blessing.

She couldn't stop reading until she finished the first chapter. Then her head was full of words that described *Isa*. He was the Word, He was Light and Life, He was flesh, the Lamb of God, the Son of God, Teacher, King, and the chapter even said He was full of grace and . . . truth. Truth? If *Isa* was full of truth, why had she never heard of Him?

⁕⁕⁕⁕⁕

Rania put the finishing touches on the last page of her sketchbook. Her hands flew smoothly over the white surface with swirls of color and abstract designs, and she skillfully hid descriptive words in colorful calligraphy along the edges and through the middle of the swirls. Descriptions of *Isa*. It eased the confusion in her mind to let it all out on paper—like tears eased the emotions that sometimes stuffed themselves into her heart. She held her work at arms length and smiled. She was getting better at this whole art thing. Maybe it was time to take the next step and trade her colored pencils in for paint.

A tap on the door broke her concentration. "Rania." Her mother opened the door. Rania's heart leapt as she realized she had forgotten to lock it when she retrieved the book. Thankfully she had already returned it to its hiding place before she began to draw.

She smiled at her mother. "Yes?"

"Father is ready for tea. He has four guests with him." Mama's eyes sparkled. "One of them is Jamal."

"OK, Mama. I'm coming."

Mama eyed Rania's sketchbook. "What's this?" She opened the door wide and walked through, holding her hands out. Rania handed her the book and held her breath. She had never shown her mother her artwork.

Mama quietly flipped through the pages, her eyes running over each picture. Rania watched for a reaction. What was Mama thinking? Would she just smile and call her a silly little girl? Would she wish Rania was smart like Halimah, who studied accounting in college? Mama continued to study the pages and Rania continued to wait. She could hear the sounds of the men cheering for *Al-Merreikh*. They must have scored a goal.

After what seemed like forever, Mama set the book down next to where Rania sat on her bed.

"Did you draw all of these?"

"Yes." Rania looked from the book up to her mother. Her brow shot up in surprise. Was Mama smiling?

"They are beautiful, Rania. You are very good at drawing."

"Thank you, Mama." Rania's heart flooded with . . . with what? Gratitude? Excitement? Happiness?

Mama squeezed Rania's shoulder and then left the room. "Don't forget to start the tea."

The door clicked shut. Rania sat stunned on the edge of her bed. For the first time in months, Mama had looked Rania in the eye and seen her. Mama had not accidentally called her Halimah. She had not sulked into her room and glanced sadly at Halimah's empty bed. Mama had seen Rania and had seen Rania's artwork . . . and had smiled.

Rania smiled back now, even though Mama was already gone. *Naematan fawq niema.* Grace in place of grace.

⁓⁓⁓⁓⁓

Rania absently kicked a stone with her shoe as she and Maysoon walked to school the next morning. It was six o'clock, and even though the temperature was already pushing passed 95 degrees, the girls relished the walk to school more than the walk home, in the midday sun with a temperature somewhere well over 100.

"Been watching soccer lately? I see you have some kicking skills. I guess you'll need to learn the rules of the game since Jamal seems to be a soccer fan."

Rania smiled at her friend. "Do you really think that Jamal visits my father because of me?"

"Of course I do," Maysoon snorted. "Why else would he spend his Friday evenings hanging out with old married men?"

"Jamal is one of Halimah's friends."

"I know."

"You don't think Father is just trying to find out about where Halimah is?"

"Honestly?"

"Yes."

Maysoon sighed. "OK, you asked for it. My father says that your father will never let Halimah come home. My father says if he ever hunts for Halimah, it will be to avenge his name."

"Oh, great, so your family just sits around and talks about my family?" Rania's agitation burst out like the firecrackers her younger brother Ali played with during Muslim festival days.

Maysoon didn't care. She shrugged. "You asked."

"I guess I did."

"Look, Rania, when your sister was caught with all those Christian books and when she told your father that she believed in *Isa*, news spread all over the neighborhood. I know that no one talks to your family about it, but we all know why she left."

"Everyone knows?"

"Of course they do. You were the gossip of the neighborhood for . . . forever."

"So why are you still my friend?"

"First of all, my mother adores your mother. She thinks the other ladies are just being stupid. And second, I don't care what people say." Maysoon laughed. "I have my own plan that just may make me the talk of the neighborhood before long."

"What are you talking about?" Rania couldn't imagine what Maysoon meant.

"I'm going to run away."

Rania stopped abruptly, inadvertently kicking a puff of dirt up in the air that dusted their blue uniform skirts in a layer of brown.

"Last week I went to the Jadeed Cultural Center and talked to the lead singer of a hip-hop group. They're going to let me perform with them at the next expo."

"What does that have to do with running away?"

"If I join a singing group, I'll have to practice with them every day. You don't think my father will let me do that, do you?" Maysoon snorted, the way she did when she was being sarcastic. "Besides, I won't really run away. I'm just going to move out."

"Don't be ridiculous, Maysoon. You can't just move out."

"Sure I can. I'll go to school all the way up to Ramadan. When school lets out for the month of fasting, I'll take the money that my father gives me to buy clothes and jewelry. I'll rent a room somewhere."

Rania could see that nothing she said would convince Maysoon otherwise. Besides, what right did she have to be a wet rag on Maysoon's hip-hop dreams, as far-fetched as they sounded? Rania wanted to be an artist, and Maysoon had done nothing but encourage her along the way. *Grace and kindness, Rania.*

She smiled at her friend and squeezed her hand as they continued walking down the street. "Well, tell me where you live, and I'll come visit you."

"I doubt it." Maysoon snorted. "You'd have to lie to your father, and you are too wimpy for that."

Rania wanted to feel hurt by Maysoon's cutting remark, but she didn't. They were just two teenage girls with fathers who were anxious to get them married off. They had to stick together.

The girls walked passed a large iron gate on their left. It was Amal's house. Her father was rich, and their house stood out like a grand mansion. Rania would almost call it an eyesore if it wasn't exactly the opposite. Amal's house looked like it had been freshly painted every day. How could a house in a dusty city like Khartoum look like that? Maybe they had servants that cleaned the walls every day.

"I haven't seen Amal lately," Rania said.

"She quit school. Her father wants her to marry before Ramadan."

"You're kidding."

"Nope. She's already begun studying the dances for her *subhia,* her bridal dance party. I think she'll begin *dukhaan* soon too." She chuckled. "Yep, she'll be sitting over sandalwood smoke and smelling like a bride before her family can utter the words *Alhamdulillah,* praise be to Allah."

"Maysoon, be careful. Don't speak of Allah irreverently like that."

"What do you care? You want to be an artist. You can't be an artist and be a good Muslim."

"Why not?"

"Number one: you are a girl. A good Muslim girl is married and pregnant. Number two: you can't be an artist because you can't draw a human face and be a good Muslim."

"I don't have to draw faces. I can draw other things."

"Well, that's true. But in any case, neither one of us are dream-come-true Muslim daughters, whether our parents realize it yet or not."

Rania kicked another stone, a little harder than she meant to this time. It stubbed her toe before thumping the wall of Amal's house.

Why couldn't she be a dream-come-true daughter?

≶ Chapter 10 ≷

Habiib had been chattering about his new baby every chance he got. Michael said sometimes he couldn't get his work done at the office because Habiib talked the whole time. His wife, Nahla, returned to her home village to give birth to their second baby. The birth had gone well, and the Sudanese couple now had a healthy baby girl.

Just as the Sudanese want it. A boy first, to prove the husband's manhood, and a girl second, so the mom has a companion around the house.

That entire week, their upcoming trip to the village to meet Nahla's family and see the baby was all Mia could think about. But the day before their trip, Michael was called into the office.

"On Friday?" Her voice was impatient. "They never work on Friday."

"After Friday prayers, the police want to come look at our office." Michael shrugged. "I can't exactly say no."

"Are you nervous?"

"No. The police have done this several times before. But I do think it's strange for them to come on their day off." Michael walked across the kitchen and looked over Mia's shoulder as she heated hot dogs in a frying pan. He pulled her away from the stove and embraced her in his strong tan arms. "I'll be fine. You and Beth can make the trip with Habiib, and you will have a great time."

"It has been a long time since I've spent time with Beth. It'll be fun to do this together."

⋙⋘

Friday morning the sun gleamed against a pristine sky, promising to shine all day long. Michael agreed to watch the kids in the morning, and they paid Tzega to come in on her day off to babysit in the afternoon when Michael was due at the office.

After her morning coffee and a quick bowl of oatmeal, Mia kissed Michael and the children and walked out to the street to meet Beth. The tall, always classy-looking nurse was sitting in the driver's seat of her

SUV with the engine running.

"Good morning, Mia. Hop in and we'll pick up Habiib at the office."

Mia settled into the passenger seat. Beth looked like a model, as usual. She wore a long brown skirt and a blue cotton long-sleeved blouse. A silky brown scarf covered her hair. Beth didn't usually cover her head, but the two ladies had agreed that for today's visit, since it was in the village, they should dress extra conservatively.

Mia, for one, was thankful for the decision. Beth's hair was almost black, but Mia's blond locks always attracted lots of attention. She covered her head with a red scarf that matched her long-sleeved blue-and-red plaid shirt and a denim skirt that was so long it dragged the ground. She felt a little like a puritanical cowgirl. *Too bad I don't have my Texas cowboy boots to finish off the outfit.*

At first Mia balked at the idea of taking Habiib on this trip without Michael, but Beth assured her that, since the two women were together, it would be OK for them to go.

"The rules are a bit different for us as foreign women," she said. "Sudanese women couldn't travel alone with a male colleague like we are doing, but no one will think anything about us doing so."

"I guess the same goes for you driving. I mean, I've never seen a Sudanese woman driving a man down the road." Mia smiled at the absurd thought.

Habiib stood outside the gate of the office when the SUV pulled up. A giant grin covered his face when he saw the ladies, and he waved happily. He hopped in the back seat of the car, and the threesome headed south out of the city. They stopped once for Habiib to buy a large bag of bread from a vendor on the side of the road.

"For my family," he said, still smiling.

Habiib assured the ladies that Nahla's home village was "just down the road a bit," but they kept driving farther and farther outside of town. On and on they drove until Habiib instructed Beth to turn left off the road.

"Finally," she muttered, turning the steering wheel.

They pulled off the road and drove over a sandy hill, which, to the ladies' surprise, brought them within view of the Nile River below.

The only clues that this might have been a place for a ferry crossing were the trucks parked on the banks. Each one was piled high with vegetables. Goats and sheep nestled together in little herds here and there. People gathered in similar groupings as they waited at the edge of a wooden ramp-looking contraption.

Beth's SUV teetered at the top of a very steep, mud-packed incline with little marshy brushes scattered here and there. Muddy water rippled at the edge and around the poles of the rickety dock. Beth and Mia stared out the front windshield in disbelief, and as they did so, an old rusty barge-type watercraft edged its way up to the ramp. The ferry had arrived.

"Does he want us to get out and ride the ferry across the river?" Mia asked Beth.

"Surely not," she whispered back. "I don't want to leave the car here, but it certainly won't fit on that ferry."

Habiib heard the hushed discussion in the front seat, and though he didn't speak English well, he must have surmised the ladies confusion, though not their dismay.

"Just drive straight down and on to the ferry," he said in a matter-of-fact tone.

"I don't think so," Beth exclaimed in English. "You want me to drive this vehicle down this cliff and somehow steer it so that we make it onto and across that rickety wooden ramp and onto the barge? Do you think I'm crazy?"

"He doesn't speak English, Beth."

"I know that, but what do you think is the probability of actually being able to get this big vehicle safely down the slippery hill and onto that floating tin can?"

Mia looked at the muddy slope before them. "Slim."

Habiib rolled down his window and recruited some onlookers to reassure the ladies. Several men, white *jallabeeyas* flapping in the breeze, leaned in and smiled, giving the international thumbs-up sign while adding some encouragement in Arabic.

"OK, OK," Beth said. "Against my better judgment, let's give it a try."

Beth put the SUV in first gear and lifted her foot off the clutch. Mia envisioned the SUV hitting a muddy spot and sliding right off the bank and into the water. She grabbed the handle of the passenger door in case she needed to throw it open and bail out. But, as the people around hollered and pointed and yelled instructions, Beth gripped the steering wheel and guided the car toward the barge until they made it down the slope, across the ramp, and onto the barge.

Disembarking on the other side was not nearly as big an ordeal, and within half an hour they paid the fees, drove off the barge and up the slope, and kept on driving.

The other side of the Nile River was arid with no buildings or paved roads in sight. Only the tire tracks in the sand marked the way. Habiib chatted happily—ignoring the fact that they had just risked life and limb to get this far. They wound around and crisscrossed in no apparent direction.

"Are we bringing you-know-who back with us? Because there is no way we will find our way back."

Beth shrugged.

Mia thought dismally of the story of Hansel and Gretel. She tried to memorize the clumps of desert brush. It was no use. Should she grab some of Habiib's newly purchased bread and scatter crumbs on the path? In reality, they were so far out that she knew they would never make it back to the ferry crossing without Habiib to guide them.

Half an hour later, a village popped up like a mirage in the desert. Sandy brown roads meandered among sandy brown walls behind which were sandy brown square houses. The streets were still just sandy brown tracks. The only contrasts in color were the inhabitants: men in bleached-white *jallabeeyas* and turbans and women in brightly colored *tobes*. One man, walking to the side of the tire tracks, turned to face the car, and Mia gasped.

He was not a coffee-skinned Arab-African man. He was white. His eyes were blue and his skin as fair as Mia's.

Mia stared out the window. "Did you see that?" Then turning to Habiib in the back seat, she asked in Arabic, "Was that man a *khawadja*?"

"Oh no, he is not a foreigner," Habiib answered. "He is Sudanese. His ancestors are from Morocco. There are a lot of people with Moroccan heritage in this village. We call them *Maghribeen*."

Habiib directed Beth to turn here and there between the sandy brown houses until they arrived at his family's home. His beautiful wife, Nahla, greeted them.

"*Min zaman ma shuftik*," Mia said. "It's been so long since I've seen you."

Nahla smiled shyly. "*Mushtagiin*." She said. "I've missed you."

"*Bilakthar*. I have missed you more." Mia smiled at Nahla. She looked fresh and beautiful. Her flowing *tobe* covered any leftover pregnancy weight. *Sudanese have a good thing going for them with these tobes. Why didn't I have a tobe when I was having babies?*

Nahla led Mia and Beth to an outhouse. "It was a long trip," she told them, "You can freshen up here."

Mia eyed the *hosh*—courtyard—that Nahla referred to. Bricks and mud walled in the back corner, leaving a space the size of a door—but with no actual door—to walk through. There was no need for a light fixture in the toilet, as there was no roof. Mia wasn't about to use the toilet outside where anyone could walk right in.

Beth grinned at Mia's wrinkled forehead. "I'll stand in the doorway with my back to you. You do your business first, and then you can stand in the doorway for me."

Relieved, Mia nodded and walked behind the wall. The packed-dirt floor matched the mud-brick walls. Mia saw the hole in the ground and a plastic container of water to the side. Regarding the hole, she wondered how everyone had such good aim. It really wasn't very big. Regarding the plastic container of water, well, Mia was not going to touch it. She had thought ahead and brought the Western version of a container of water . . . toilet paper.

<hr />

Mia and Beth spent most of the day with Habiib's family. They met many relatives and neighbors and ate lots of food together. Mia was most excited to hold Nahla's six-week-old baby. She was tiny and beautiful. Black kohl eyeliner traced her big round eyes. Mia thought it made her look like an ancient Egyptian baby. Nahla had tied a cloth pouch of black cumin seeds around her little wrist.

"What is that for?" Mia asked Beth. Beth would know things like that. She spent many hours every week with Sudanese people when she worked in the refugee camps. She was well acquainted with Sudanese customs. Mia loved that about Beth, but it also made her jealous. Beth had helped Mia break out of her fear of a culture so different than her own and helped her meet other Sudanese people. Mia was learning to become satisfied in her own role as mother and wife, but sometimes she still fought envy toward Beth, who was single and had plenty of time to hang out with Sudanese, study Arabic, and do whatever she wanted.

"That's to ward away evil," Beth said.

Mia looked at Nahla. Surely Nahla didn't believe that a tiny pouch of black seeds was going to keep evil away. She looked at Beth, who was quiet. "Are you worried about evil?" Mia asked Nahla.

Beth mumbled something.

"What?"

"This isn't a good time," she repeated quietly.

"Why not?" Mia asked.

"Look around, there are a lot of women in here."

"So?"

"Yes," Nahla answered Mia. "We all worry about evil."

"Do you know what I do?" Mia felt Beth's glare, but she forged ahead. "I pray in the name of *Isa*. Have you heard of Him?"

"Yes."

"Oh? You have? That's good. What have you heard?"

Just then the little baby began to cry.

"I think she's hungry," Nahla said as she reached for her daughter.

Mia handed her back carefully. At least the conversation was open. Maybe there would be time to get back to it later. She glanced at Beth whose lips were pursed, as if trying to keep herself from speaking.

➣ Chapter 11 ➣

By midafternoon Beth was getting antsy.

"Nahla, it was so wonderful to see you and the new baby. Mia and I really need to go home now, so we can be in Khartoum by dark."

Nahla smiled. "Yes, a little bit later."

A little bit later, Habiib stepped into the room where all the women were to check on his wife and visitors. His beaming smile proclaimed pride over his new baby and beautiful wife. Mia wondered if this would be a good time to bring up *Isa* again. After all, Habiib had already mentioned to Michael that he wanted Nahla to hear all about it.

She looked over at Beth who was getting increasingly agitated. Maybe now was not the best time. Beth stood and insisted to Habiib, "We have to go home now."

"The ferry will not run again today. You'll have to wait until tomorrow," Habiib said.

Mia looked at him in disbelief. What was he talking about?

"What? Oh, no, we can't do that." She turned to Nahla, hoping to find sympathy from a fellow mother. "I have children of my own back home. Surely you understand, I have to get home today."

Mia's throat was dry. Her stomach churned. There was no cell phone coverage this far away from the city. How could she get word back to Michael about what was going on? As far as he knew, the ladies were in a nearby village and would be home any minute. The reality was that they were in some desert village across the river and hours away with no means of getting home.

Mia looked at Beth and whispered in English, "How could Habiib do this to us? He should have told us hours ago so that we could make the last ferry."

"Habiib, this is not fair," Beth said. Her voice sounded calm but firm. "There has to be a way to get home today."

Habiib smiled and shrugged. "This is Sudan. If the ferry doesn't run, you have no other way to go back."

Mia looked around the room at Habiib and Nahla and the cousins and neighbors who whittled the hot afternoon away by staring at Beth and Mia.

"OK," Mia said to everyone in general. Her desperation turned to determination. "We will just drive home alone. I will swim across the river, if I have to. But I am going home to my husband and children today."

Mia heard the ridiculous words as they came out of her mouth and hung in the room. She thought the hosts must think she was an idiot, given that the American ladies had no clue how to even get out of the village.

Habiib looked at Mia with a thoughtful smirk on his face. "Your Arabic is getting very good."

Mia wanted to smack him across the face and scream, "Focus, Habiib! We are talking about how to get me home, not how my Arabic has improved."

But before she could embarrass herself with another rant, Habiib sighed and gave up the charade. "The ferry runs until dark," he admitted. "If we leave now, we can still make it."

He reluctantly told the women in the room that he and the guests would be returning to Khartoum. Several of the older ladies clucked disapprovingly, but Mia didn't care.

Mia and Beth made a final trip to the outhouse, going together so that they could take turns standing guard. They drank the cups of water offered to them and thanked their hosts for the hospitality. They tried to be polite but rushed through the good-byes, determined to make it to the ferry before dark.

The ladies were ushered to the front of the house to wait for Habiib, who was apparently grabbing some last minute things from the back of the house. The front part of the house belonged to Nahla's parents. The large room, which was really more of a veranda than a room, opened to the front courtyard. It was open-air with a pleasant breeze.

Mia noticed most of the family sat with them. Knowing that they'd be leaving soon, Mia felt more relaxed and carried on conversation with a couple of the ladies who sat near her. She even got to hold the baby one last time.

At a lull in the conversation, Beth leaned over to Mia. "It's been a long time, this is weird."

"I know," Mia said. "It seems like Habiib should be ready by now."

Mia surveyed the room. All the family was there: Nahla's parents, siblings, cousins, and the baby. Every member of the family was there . . . except Habiib and Nahla.

The baby is six weeks old. Six weeks after the birth of the baby is enough time for a new mother to heal . . .

Mia gasped and leaned toward her companion. "Beth, this was not an invitation to come meet Habiib's in-laws."

"What do you mean?" Beth asked.

"This was a free ride home for his first spousal visit since his baby was born. You do realize that everyone, and I mean everyone, except Habiib and Nahla are here don't you? Look around." Her friend glanced around the room. "You know what we are waiting for, don't you?"

"You can't be serious?"

"Oh, yes, I'm totally serious."

"Ooooh, I'm so mad at him. I thought he wanted us to meet his family."

No one on the veranda could understand the English conversation taking place. The people simply grinned at the American ladies and continued to coo over the new baby.

A few minutes later Habiib and Nahla showed up. Habiib held a bag in his hand, and Nahla had a silly grin on her face.

As promised, a ferry was available to take the three travelers back across the Nile. Beth drove in silence, so Mia tried to make small talk with Habiib.

"It was great to see Nahla again," she said in Arabic.

"Yeah, I bet that's what he's saying too." Beth muttered under her breath.

Unlike Beth, Mia found the whole escapade kind of funny. She looked through the rearview mirror at Habiib. He looked happy and peaceful, just staring out the window. It was obvious he was not bothered by Beth's refusal to speak to him.

When they were close to Khartoum, cell phone reception returned. Mia sent Michael a text to let him know she was later than expected, but would be home before too long.

As she hit send, she remembered how Michael would text or call her to say that he would be late getting home from work. Mia usually got mad or, at the very least, frustrated about it.

But my situation is completely out of my control. I tried to leave the village earlier.

Wasn't that the same with Michael? It wasn't always his fault that he was late. There were probably many instances that the situation was out of his control.

I need to be more gracious to Michael.

⇒ Chapter 12 ⇐

Only after waving good-bye to Beth and walking inside the privacy gate to her house did Mia realized how exhausted she felt.

She opened the front door and walked inside. Michael walked out of the kitchen, drying his hands on a towel.

Has he been washing dishes?

"Welcome back." He gave Mia a hug.

"Uh, you may not want to hug me. I'm sweaty."

Michael stepped back and chuckled. "It's Sudan, Mia. We're all sweaty."

Mia laughed. "Where are the kids?"

"In bed already, but they want you to tell them good night."

Mia had deeply enjoyed her day away, even if their host had ulterior motives for the visit. But no amount of adventure outside the home could replace the joy of returning to her children. She missed them all day and feeling their soft cheeks as she kissed them good night was a better reward than a thousand days spent outside her home.

After telling the children good night, Mia walked into the living room. She began talking before she'd actually even entered the room. "You won't believe the day I had. Can you guess what Habiib did? Well, I don't think you'll be able to. But guess anyways. Go ahead. Oh, never mind, I'll tell you. He wanted to sleep with his wife. And he invited us because he had no other way to get to the village unless we brought him. Can you imagine? Isn't that the craziest thing?"

Mia plopped on the couch beside her husband and finally noticed Michael's strained face. He was listening to her, but Mia could tell it was taking a lot of effort.

"What's wrong? Oh, I know. You're mad at me for being late, aren't you? I tried to call earlier, but there was no cell phone coverage. And then Habiib lied to us and said there was no ferry. Oh, yeah, this so-called 'nearby village' was on the other side of the Nile. We had to take a ferry." Mia stopped and gasped. "Is that it, Michael? Are you mad at me?"

"Mad at you? No, of course not. It's not you. I just had a strange conversation at the office today. I can't stop thinking about it."

"Oh . . . the police came today." Mia had completely forgotten about the appointment with the police at Michael's office. At least she remembered now. "So, what happened?"

"Well, they asked some questions about our projects, and they took one of the computers 'in order to read over the documents' they said."

"So, is that bad?"

"Well, there's nothing on the computer that they aren't welcome to read. I think they just want to find a way to confiscate the computer, it's one of the nicer ones we had shipped in from the States. But that's not what's bothering me. It's actually something a co-worker said after the police left. Jeff, you know the guy who is here from Dallas for a couple of months, he heard my conversation with Habiib last week."

"And?"

"And he told me that after Habiib and I left, he noticed some of the guys in the office talking to each other. Of course, he can't speak Arabic, so he didn't know what they were saying. But their manner struck him as odd. Then one of them made a phone call. He stepped out of the room, so Jeff doesn't know who he called."

"It could be nothing, right? I mean, Jeff is a new guy."

"Yes, it could be nothing. But Jeff's been around the block a time or two. This is not his first overseas job. He knows the kinds of things to look for. Anyway, he told me I needed to be careful what I said in the office. He thinks that when I was sharing about the Bible and Jesus with Habiib, I may have upset some of the other guys in the office."

"So a couple of guys don't like what you believe. What does that matter?"

"Well, Jeff thinks the phone call was to the police. He thinks that's why they came today. Like maybe there had been previous communication with the police."

"Oh."

"We may have just lost one of our best computers, and now we have the police looking over our shoulder at a time when they are already scrutinizing organizations like ours."

With the kids, Mia was always able to fix the problem: a Band-Aid, a hug, a piece of candy. Her mommy-solutions would not fix this problem. She stared at the floor, absently twisting a sweaty lock of hair around her finger.

"So are you going to stop sharing with Habiib?"

"No. He already told me he wanted to hear more, so I want to share more. But I'll try to find a time when we aren't in the office."

"I wanted to talk to Nahla about Jesus today, but Beth got upset. Do you think it has to do with all of this?"

"Yep. Beth definitely thinks we shouldn't be sharing in the office."

"But I wasn't in the office."

"Right, but you are sharing with Habiib's wife. So she's connected."

"I don't understand. Beth used to be so excited about sharing with anyone. I mean, she's the one who first gave a copy of the New Testament to our friend Abbas."

"Yes, but Abbas doesn't work with Kellar Hope. I think Beth is afraid to put the foundation at risk, and she thinks we should keep work separate from spiritual things."

"Well, maybe she's right. If you keep your head down at work, at least you'd have a job and we could just share about Jesus with other people, people who don't make decisions about if we can stay here or not."

"Maybe. You think so? What about Habiib's interest? He wants me to share more."

"Habiib could be telling the police about us. I mean, he was dishonest with me today. What if he's faking interest so that you'll keep sharing?"

"Maybe." Michael sounded doubtful.

"You don't want to be the guy who shut down Kellar Hope Foundation."

"No, I don't."

"So just find someone else to share with rather than Habiib. This whole thing will blow over."

"Maybe."

He was beginning to sound like a broken record.

⇒ Chapter 13 ⇐

Rania tried to subdue her excitement. But her eyes danced and she couldn't hide her smile. Jadeed Cultural Center was hosting an art expo in just two weeks—obviously trying to squeeze in the event before everything halted for Ramadan, the holy month of fasting. Maysoon said the expo would feature music, drama, art, and handicrafts. She put in a good word for Rania and snagged an invitation for her to enter two drawings in the art competition.

Rania must keep the event a secret, of course. She trembled at the thought of her father finding out. She could hear his deep, stern voice in her head. "That cultural center is a den of Western propaganda. No good Muslim should set foot there."

Would she have to start down a path of lying in order to follow her dream? She didn't want to. *Mama liked my drawings. Maybe she will agree to let me do it.*

Rania sighed and stuffed her sketchbook into the oversized handbag. She grabbed a *tarha* from a hook on the back of her bedroom door and stopped in front of the mirror to wrap the scarf neatly over her hair, securing it by tucking the edge under at her chin.

As she opened her bedroom door and stepped out, Ali came barreling by, nearly knocking her over right in the hallway.

"Hey, watch out. What's your rush?"

At 13, Ali was clumsy and still a bit childish. He was stocky like their mother. Rania's little brother carried an arrogance about him as if he were a little king.

"I am thirsty, just coming inside for a drink." His dark face was flushed, obviously from running around outside.

"Why don't you just drink from the clay jars on the street? That's what they are there for. Then you won't get the house smelly from all your sweat."

"Because . . ." Ali stopped and let his words come out long and whiny while his eyes twinkled. "I want some *karkaday*. That's more refreshing. Will you make me some?"

"Hibiscus tea? Right now? I'm headed out the door."

"It won't take long. Come on, you can do it and then go."

Rania sighed and followed her brother to the kitchen. Sure, he was a brat sometimes, but she loved him. All little brothers were brats, right?

Ali sat on a chair at the small kitchen table while Rania set her purse on the countertop and retrieved a glass jar from the shelf above it. The clear jar that previously held jelly was recycled to hold dried hibiscus flower petals. They were dark red and, at a glance, looked black. They twisted and curled about each other and crackled quietly as Rania dipped a spoon in the jar and fished out enough of the flowers to cover the bottom of a small kettle. She poured water on top and sat it on the hob, lighting a flame and adjusting the heat.

"Make it sweet, Rania. I like lots of sugar. Make it sweet, like Jamaaaaaaaaal." Ali cackled.

Had Father been talking about Jamal? Or had Ali also noticed that the tall handsome college-mate of Halimah's had been visiting more often lately?

"What do you mean?" Rania tried to sound oblivious.

"Don't be stupid, Rania. Jamal doesn't even like soccer. Do you really think he comes here because he wants to watch soccer?"

"Well, yes," Rania said honestly. *What Sudanese man doesn't like soccer?*

"Silly girl." Ali's words were condescending as he spoke to his older sister. Rania resisted the urge to demand respect from him. It wasn't her place. He'd learn respect later, when he was older. "Jamal is here for you. I've heard him and Father talk about you more than once when he's over here. But I don't like it."

Rania eyed him as she spooned heaps of sugar into a plastic pitcher. "Why not?"

"Because if you get married and leave, who will make me *karkaday*?" Ali laughed at his own teasing.

Rania pulled a handful of ice cubes out of the freezer and plunked them into a glass for Ali. She took one cube and tossed it at her brother playfully. It missed him and landed on the floor by his feet, where it immediately melted on the hot tile. Ali smirked.

The water in the kettle began to bubble. Rania was in a hurry, so she hoped the dried *karkaday* had steeped to Ali's satisfaction. She poured the hot liquid through a sieve over the sugar, stirring to mix the refreshing concoction.

Jamal's not a bad guy. Maybe he would make a good husband. If he was friends with Halimah, maybe he knows where she is. Maybe he understands why she went away.

A short while later, Rania slipped out the front door and onto the dust-filled street. Ali's friends hovered under a neem tree, where three large jars of water sat on metal frames in the shade. Each jar had a faucet toward the bottom and a metal cup attached to a long string. As was custom, anyone could drink from the clay jars. These particular ones were owned by Rania's family and were seen as a beautiful act of charity. Burlap bags draped the outsides of the jars and periodic dousing with water helped to keep the water inside cool.

The boys spotted Rania and one of them called to her. "Ya, Rania, where is Ali?"

"He's coming, boys. Just be patient."

"Where are you going?" Another boy called.

"None of your business," Rania returned. But she grinned as she did so. These were the neighborhood boys. She'd watched them grow up and she knew each family well. In Khartoum one's family and one's neighbors were intimately knitted into life. Everyone knew just about everything about everyone else.

Rania turned left and walked down the street toward Maysoon's house. Today they would look through her drawings and decide which two she should enter into the art competition.

Rania was eager to see Maysoon do whatever it was she did as part of the hip-hop group. Maysoon was so secretive. She kept telling Rania to wait and watch her perform at the expo.

After the ten-minute walk in the stifling heat of the afternoon, Rania was parched and ready for a drink. Maysoon's house did not have clay jars outside. No matter, a large glass of water would be the first thing her friend would offer her upon arrival.

She reached up and pressed the button for the doorbell. It was installed high in the wall beside the privacy gate that surrounded Maysoon's house so that young school children wouldn't walk by and ring it just to be naughty.

Maysoon had two older and five younger siblings. Her house was usually full of activity, and for a fleeting moment Rania thought it strange that she could not hear the patter of feet in the courtyard on the other side of the gate.

A few moments later Maysoon opened the gate and ushered Rania in. She wasn't smiling and she only whispered, "*Salaam aleykum*, welcome."

"What's wrong?" Rania's heart pounded in her chest.

Maysoon sank onto a metal bed just inside the gate—a common piece of furniture in Sudanese courtyards because it doubled as a place to sleep in the cool of the night and a place to relax in the heat of the day. She grabbed Rania's arm and pulled her down beside her.

Rania heard a noise coming from inside the house. Someone was crying. Was it Maysoon's mother?

"It's about Amal," Maysoon said.

"Amal from school? What about her?"

Maysoon brought her finger to her lips. "Shhh, not so loud. I want to hear what Mother is saying."

Rania strained her ears. The crying had stopped, and a voice could be heard talking on the phone. The name of a hospital. The name of a doctor. Rania's eyes met Maysoon's in confusion.

"Amal tried to kill herself," Maysoon whispered. "She drank *hibir* from the henna."

Rania gasped. *Hibir* was the black ink mixed with dried henna leaves that made the beautiful swirls of designs on the hands and feet of Sudanese brides and wives.

The substance that created beauty on the outside was a poison that could destroy the inside.

"What do we do?" Rania's eyes pleaded for an answer. Maysoon had life figured out. She was brave and strong. She was like Halimah.

"I don't know. We wait, I guess." Maysoon's wobbly voice did not comfort Rania.

They sat side by side on the bed in the sun. Rania forgot how thirsty she was, and she ignored the sweat rolling down her spine.

The girls heard Maysoon's mother hang up the phone and scurry about the house. Perhaps she was headed to the hospital? Maysoon didn't move, so Rania didn't either.

The phone rang and Maysoon's mother answered it. A wail filled the space between the girls and the older woman. Tears streamed down Maysoon's face and Rania knew what had happened. Amal was gone.

Rania thought of Amal's body lying in a hospital bed. It would smell faintly of sandalwood, as Amal had already begun the daily beautifying treatments for her wedding. The large amount of *hibir* and henna her family must have purchased for her henna party did not grace her arms and legs as her mother planned. It stained her throat and stomach like black tar.

Had Amal really been that sad? Rania's heart ached as she remembered that less than a year ago her own family thought Halimah had killed herself. In their frantic search for Rania's big sister, they called every hospital and clinic, sure they would discover her body there.

Rania remembered the night that Halimah called home. What a relief to know her sister was alive. She had cried all that night, but it was not sadness.

Today was sadness. Today was death. Death was so final. Death was a slap in the face. And suicide? Well, that was shameful for Amal's family. Rania thought of Amal's grand house, just down the street from her own. It didn't matter how many servants washed the walls of the mansion. No amount of water could wash the shame of suicide.

Rania walked home slowly. She was beginning to dehydrate, but she didn't care. She'd left Maysoon to help her mother and younger siblings. Rania's own mother would be receiving a phone call at any moment, so it was best for her to go back home.

She turned the corner onto her street and felt choked by the silence. The boys were gone from the jars of water. Neighbors were shut behind their own privacy gates. Rania knew that soon the street would be flooded with mourners as Amal's body was brought home and prepared for burial.

According to Muslim custom, she would be buried quickly. Mourning lasted for several days. By tomorrow a tent would be erected outside Amal's large home for the *bika*, the mourning ceremony.

Would the neighborhood know that Amal's death was suicide? Would her family make up a story instead, like a traffic accident or an illness? Would Allah forgive Amal?

Rania arrived at the gate of her own house, much smaller than Amal's. She fished through her handbag until she found the key and then twisted it in the lock. She opened the gate, and as she did, her mother's wails filled the courtyard.

ꙮ Chapter 14 ꙮ

Aflurry of activity filled the following days in Rania's neighborhood. The official word was that Amal had died of an allergic reaction to henna. No one suggested, except in hushed tones behind closed doors, that the henna dye had been ingested.

Amal's mother and sisters washed her body and wrapped it in the traditional white burial cloth. The same day that she died, the *sheikh* from the local mosque performed the *salaat al-janazah*, the funeral prayer. He asked Allah to increase Amal's good works and to forgive her bad works.

Amal's family sat in mourning. Some of them sat under the tent and some in the cavernous house. The other families of the neighborhood brought food for them. Visitors were kind and gentle to the family, even though they also contributed to the gossip that bubbled just under the surface.

Rania brought food to Amal's house on the second day of mourning. Her arms strained under the weight of the giant pot of stew Mama cooked that morning. A large bag of bread balanced precariously atop the pot as she walked gingerly down the street, careful not to tip the pot and spill its contents.

As she approached the whitewashed walls, she saw Haj Azeez, Amal's fiancé, arrive in his old Mercedes. He eased his aging body out of the car and made his way to the tent where all the men sat. As Rania neared the front door, she overheard the man speaking to Amal's father. The men were about the same age, and, both wearing *jalla-beeyas*, they looked like brothers.

"*Inna lillaahi wa inna ilayhi raaji'oon,*" Haj Azeez was saying, "To Allah we belong and to him we return."

"*Al baraka feekoom,*" Amal's father replied. "Blessings on you."

Where is the blessing in this? Rania ducked her head and walked past the men and into the house half wondering if they could hear her thoughts. She knew that Haj Azeez was only saying what was appropriate at a time like this. But Amal was going to be his second wife, and she

74

couldn't help but wonder how long it would take Haj Azeez to find a replacement.

At week's end, the tent was down and life was mostly back to normal. Amal's mother still wore black, as she would for the next 40 days.

After missing two days of school to help Amal's family, Rania and Maysoon kept their minds occupied with their studies and with talk about the upcoming expo at the cultural center.

"It is less than a week away now," said Maysoon, as they walked to school together early on a Sunday morning, the first day of the school week. Her gaze drifted to the giant clean walls as they walked by Amal's house.

"So much bad luck."

"What do you mean?"

Rania sighed. "Amal . . . Halimah . . . why is it all happening in our neighborhood?"

"Allah is merciful, that's what my mother says. He has willed all of these things to happen. There is nothing we can do."

The girls walked in silence for a few minutes before Rania spoke again. "So, the expo is Friday. I still don't know how to get permission from Father."

"I do," Maysoon replied. "I told my mother that you and I are so sad about Amal. That's true; it's not even a lie. I asked if you can come stay with me on Friday night. All you have to do is ask your father for permission to come to my house. You don't have to lie because you don't have to tell him what we are doing."

"But what about Jamal? He always comes to visit Father on Fridays, and I know I'll be expected to serve tea."

Maysoon sighed in unhidden frustration. "I can't work everything out for you, Rania. Sometimes you just have to take a stand for yourself."

***

Rania needn't have worried about Jamal's visit. When she returned from school in the afternoon, her parents informed her they were leaving on Thursday to drive to Wad Medani and visit Haboba, Rania's grandmother, for a few days.

"You can stay here or come with us," Father said. "Abdu and Ali will be here."

"What if I stay here but sleep at Maysoon's house?" Rania asked.

"That sounds like a good idea," he replied. "Maysoon has a respectable family. Yes, her father is very religious. You may stay with her."

"Thank you, Father." Rania smiled broadly. Was she acting overly excited?

"By the way," Father said, "Jamal is coming by later to bring me something. I won't be here. Can you collect it from him for me?"

"Yes, Father. Sure."

<hr />

Just before sunset, Father, Abdu, and Ali went to prayers at the mosque. Rania swept the rough cement in the courtyard and listened to the call of the minaret echoing down the dust-filled street. Voices mingled as men and boys walked briskly toward the square building with the tall minaret.

"*Allahu akbar. Allahu akbar.* Allah is great. Allah is great." The words twirled in Rania's mind. She'd heard them five times a day for as long as she could remember. Indeed, God was great.

"*Ashadu an la ilaha illa Allah.* I bear witness that there is no god except the One God." She stood in the courtyard, and for the first time she let the words pierce into her heart. She agreed with the *muezzin*, the man who called from the minaret.

"*Ashadu anna Mohammadan Rasool Allah.* I bear witness that Mohammad is the messenger of God." Rania's brow wrinkled. Was it true? If Mohammed was the messenger of God, then who was *Isa*, who she had been reading about in Halimah's book?

The third chapter of the little book gripped her. "One and only Son": that's who *Isa* was. If He really was the "one and only," shouldn't she be learning more about Him? She determined to read more of the little book. If it didn't have answers to Halimah's whereabouts, perhaps it had answers for Rania's deeper questions.

The gossip about Rania's family and Halimah's disappearance were finally replaced by the shameful secrets of Amal's death. Meanwhile Maysoon threatened to run away from home, and here was Rania, pursuing art, which she knew her father would never approve of. What was it all for? Freedom? Was that what everyone wanted?

No. Freedom was only part of it. It was more than that. Peace. It was peace. Did Halimah have peace? Did Amal?

Rania sighed and looked up toward the softening sky. She wanted peace. Would Allah show her the way?

The final words from the minaret rang out over the neighborhood. "*Allahu Akbar. Allahu Akbar. La ilaha illa Allah.*"

⁕⁕⁕

A rap on the metal gate told Rania that Jamal had arrived with his delivery for Father. Mama rattled pots and pans in the kitchen and didn't hear the knocking.

Rania opened the gate. "*Salaam aleykum.*"

"*Aleykum wassalaam.*" Jamal's tall figure was a silhouette against the orange streetlight. Rania's heart skipped a beat. He was definitely a handsome man. His broad shoulders and strong jawline suggested confidence. His eyes were kind and his smile contagious.

He didn't move from where he stood just outside Rania's gate. She knew he was a respectable man and would never suggest entering a house when the men of the house were gone.

"Here is a magazine I promised to give to your father. It has an article about *Al-Merreikh*, his soccer team." Jamal held the glossy periodical with one hand and pointed to the cover with the other. A player posed on the front with *Al-Merreikh's* uniform and a shiny soccer ball in his hands.

Rania remembered Ali's comment about Jamal. Was it true that he did not really like soccer?

Jamal glanced casually from side to side. Then he coughed and spoke in a low voice. "Can I ask you a question? It will probably sound strange."

Rania's brow wrinkled but she remained silent.

"Look, I'm taking a big risk here. I just want to ask you: have you ever had a dream? I mean a dream that told you to do something?"

Rania could hardly believe she was having this conversation. Maybe Halimah talked like this with her college friends, but Rania was not so bold. Besides, she was only 16.

"I think you need to talk to Father about this . . . if it's about marriage, I mean."

Jamal's tense face broke into a giant smile, and Rania felt her insides melting.

"No, Rania, I'm not talking about marriage. I'm talking about a dream. I had a dream. I think it has to do with what Halimah was caught up in."

"Why are you telling me this?"

"Are you searching for answers too?"

Does he know about the book? "*Astaghfir Allah.* Allah, forgive me." Rania muttered under her breath.

"Are you?" Jamal pressed.

Her life was over. She'd be joining Amal in the ranks of the deceased soon. "Yes," she squeaked. She closed her eyes, waiting for the impact of the first rock from her stoning. She was as good as dead, and it terrified her.

"Hey." Rania felt a tap on her hand. "Hey." She opened her eyes and realized Jamal was tapping her hand with the magazine. "Take this. Quit looking like I'm torturing you. No one has heard us."

Rania looked around. The gate was wide open. Jamal stood outside and she stood inside. No one was on the street. She wasn't being stoned. She allowed herself to smile slightly. She had just confessed to Jamal that she was searching for answers, and he had sort of confessed the same to her. And they were both still alive.

Hadn't she been taught since she was an infant never to question her religion? Hadn't she been raised to recite prayers and verses and bow in worship and offer her heart to Allah and never ask why?

What was so dangerous about wanting to know why? Couldn't she look for answers? Wasn't Allah big enough to withstand her questions?

Jamal spoke again. "I had a dream. I told Halimah. I never did anything else about it after that. But since Halimah left, I've had more dreams." He glanced up and down the street one more time. "Look, I think your father wants you and me to get married. I want you to know that if we do, we can look for answers together."

Rania looked into Jamal's eyes. She never looked straight into a man's eyes before. It felt very intimate. She could love Jamal. She could marry him. Even at 16. And if Jamal would let her keep reading the book . . . and if Jamal would let her speak of Halimah as if she had not disappeared forever . . .

"I have a book," Rania whispered.

"Like what Halimah had?"

"I think so."

"Don't let your father find it, Rania."

"Should I get rid of it?" Rania didn't want to, but she was so transfixed by Jamal's eyes that she would do anything he said right about now.

"No, you should read it. Just don't let your father see it. I better go now. *Masa 'ilxayr*, good afternoon." Jamal turned and walked away.

"*Masa 'innoor*," Rania returned the greeting, "Light afternoon." She held the magazine tight against her chest as she watched his figure fade away.

⇒ Chapter 15 ⇐

I'm going to start running for exercise," Michael said.

Mia took a sip of the coffee to buy a little time to hide her surprise.

"Wow. You haven't exercised since we moved to Sudan."

"I know, and it's driving me crazy. I need to be able to think clearly, and I just can't when I sit in an office all day."

"But in this heat? Honey, it's over 100 degrees every day. You'll have heatstroke."

"I'll run early. If I run at five, I can still get home and take a shower before you and I meet to read the Bible."

Oh, brother, more time away from home. Mia took a second sip of the steamy beverage and forced herself to say, "I think it's a great idea."

"Good morning." Mia and Michael turned from where they sat at the dining room table to see the kids standing in the doorway, pajama-clad and sleepy-eyed.

"Well, good morning." Mia grinned. "You are all up early on a Saturday."

"We wanted to see you, Mom," Corey said.

"Did you come tell us goodnight last night?" Annie asked.

"I did, but all three of you were already asleep."

"Did you give us kisses, Mommy?" Dylan asked as he crawled into Mia's lap.

"Why, yes I did." She said, giving Dylan a squeeze. "Just like this." She gave him a big kiss on his cheek. Dylan's blond curls bounced as he giggled and squirmed.

"What are we going to do today?" Corey asked. He sat at the table beside his father. Mia looked at the two. Corey was a miniature version of Michael. He was getting taller, and his skin was getting dark, just like his father's.

"Well," Michael said, setting his coffee mug on the table, "Abbas has already called to invite us to lunch at his house." Michael looked at Mia as he said this, searching for permission from her.

"Wow," she replied, "he called early. It's not even eight o'clock yet."

"I know," Michael said. "I guess he was trying to catch us before we planned anything."

"I guess you told him yes?"

Michael grinned and shrugged. "I didn't know what else to say."

"Mr. Abbas is fun," Corey said. "I like playing with Yusra."

Mia relented. She'd wanted to relax at home after spending the whole previous day with Habiib's in-laws, but Corey's enthusiasm was contagious. Plus, she'd still get to spend the day with Michael.

Michael said they wouldn't leave until about four in the afternoon, the typical lunchtime in Sudan. Tzega would come to work at nine and probably be done by the early afternoon, so all the housework would be finished. As the day unfolded, Mia became more excited about visiting with Abbas's wife, Widad.

When Mia first met Abbas, she and Beth were buying food at his little neighborhood shop. Beth had given him a copy of the New Testament, and he had been reading it diligently.

"It talks so much about love," he commented to Mia. Since Beth was single, it was not appropriate for her to visit Abbas, so Mia and Michael began a friendship with the young family. The kids loved to visit because their young daughter Yusra always took them out to the quiet dirt roads outside the house to play with the other kids in the neighborhood.

Letting the kids wander the streets would have terrified Mia when they first moved to Khartoum. But now that they'd lived here for a couple of years, she knew that the kids were actually very safe out in the neighborhood. Everyone within half a mile knew that they were the *khawadja* family that came to visit Abbas and Widad.

<hr />

At four o'clock the Westons piled into their SUV and headed across town. In the spirit of true Sudanese hospitality, Abbas and Widad greeted them as if they were long-lost friends. Even Yusra came running out to the side of the road where they parked.

Everyone shook hands. Michael reached his right arm to Abbas's left shoulder while Abbas did the same to him, and they ended in a handshake. Mia touched her cheeks against Widad's cheeks, back and forth several times as was customary for women who were close friends. By the time they'd finished their greetings, Yusra had Dylan by the hand and was walking off down the street.

"Yusra. Come back," her mother called. "Let them drink something first."

The pudgy little girl with tiny braids all over her head reluctantly returned, and they all walked through the gate in the mud wall and entered the first courtyard of their home.

Unlike Hanaan's modern house, Widad's house was very simple. The courtyard was small with an outhouse on the right, an entrance to the shop on the left, and an opening to the back courtyard just past the shop. Opposite the outer gate in the first courtyard was a small kitchen. It was dark in the room, but Mia could see pots and pans piled onto a makeshift cabinet that was formerly a metal bed frame. The walls around the court-yards were made of mud brick and were just low enough so that if Mia were on her tiptoes, she would be able to see into the neighbor's courtyard.

The back courtyard was about the same size as the front one, some 20 square feet. One room opened onto this packed-dirt open area. It was the bedroom that Abbas, Widad, and Yusra shared. From former visits, Mia knew that the room was just big enough to hold a queen-size bed and a wardrobe.

In the back courtyard there were five metal chairs and a matching metal table. Sun-faded cushions lined the seats and backs of the chairs. This is where Widad ushered the family before she disappeared to the kitchen in the first courtyard.

A few minutes later she returned with a tray holding bottles of soda. Dylan's eyes grew large and he looked at Mia.

"Is one of those for me?"

Mia glared at him, trying to telepathically instruct him to be quiet. She knew the family could not afford to give them these drinks. If they knew Dylan was so pleased, they'd give him two. Sudanese Arabs were hospitable that way. "What did he say?" Widad asked in Arabic, as she set the tray on the metal table.

Mia grinned. "Oh, he just said you are so nice." *Is lying OK when it is more polite than the truth?*

"Well then, *habeebee*, this one if for you." Widad took a bottle of Coke and handed it to Dylan's outstretched arms.

"*Shukran*," Dylan squealed, "Thank you."

Well, at least he's appreciative.

The children, including Yusra, each got a bottle of soda, as did Michael and Mia. Abbas and Widad did not drink any.

"I'm too fat." Abbas laughed as he leaned back in his metal chair and rubbed his belly.

Widad hurried off to the kitchen again and returned with an enormous tray containing fried meat, a plate of dark chunks mixed with peppers (Mia guessed it was liver), a plate of sliced tomatoes, cucumber, and carrots, and a plate of fried potatoes. Between all the plates were small loaves of bread that looked like hot dog buns.

"Widad," Michael exclaimed. "This has worn you out."

"It's nothing more than my simple responsibility," she said, but her eyes danced.

Dylan, who had already managed to spill Coke down the front of his shirt, called to his siblings playing in the front courtyard. "Corey, Annie, there's food."

The kids came running to the table. Everyone gathered around the large tray.

"Abbas," Michael said. "You have blessed our family with your hospitality. May I thank God for this meal?"

"Yes. Of course," Abbas said.

He looked at Michael as if he was not sure what Michael would do next. Mia didn't know either. She'd never heard Michael offer to pray with a Muslim before a meal. Normally they just thanked the Lord in their hearts. She'd even told her children to do the same. But things were different now. Now that they'd been reading Acts. Now that their time in Sudan may be cut short.

Michael looked down at the tray of food. He left his eyes open and said, "Lord, we thank You for this food that You have provided. We thank You for friends. In Jesus' name I pray."

He looked across the tray at Abbas and smiled. Abbas smiled back. The impromptu prayertime wasn't awkward. It was actually nice. Abbas seemed happy, and he urged them to eat, which they all did with gusto. Mia thought about her dad in the hospital. If she had gone back to Texas to be with her parents, this might not have happened. Her mom was right, it was better for her to stay in Sudan.

∿∿∿

The next day, Beth visited, and Mia relayed the story over cups of tea on the front veranda. Beth smiled. "That's great, Mia."

"I know. And before we left, Abbas told Michael that he should pray before all our meals together. And not only that, he kept bringing up things he'd read in the copy of the New Testament that you gave him."

"You know, I think Abbas and Widad are definitely people you should invest in. I think it's great that you are being so bold with them. I think you should focus on them and not so much on Habiib."

"You know, Beth, I've thought about that. But I just don't agree. If Habiib is interested, we should keep talking to him about Jesus."

"Habiib is associated with Kellar Hope. Since our office is under fire from the government, we don't need to be flirting with any kind of extra trouble."

Mia sat up straight in her chair, indignant. "How is sharing about Christ the same as flirting with trouble?" She wondered if Tzega could hear them from the living room where she was dusting.

Beth calmly took a sip of tea, unaffected by the awkward silence as Mia waited for her answer. "I just think you and Michael need to be careful sharing Jesus' love and even giving Bibles to friends—all of that is good stuff. But think of all the good things Kellar Hope is already doing. Do you really want to risk shutting down the foundation because of your actions?"

Mia frowned at Beth. She wanted to come back with a strong statement, but words eluded her. How could her friend, who loved Jesus dearly, say that they should pick and choose who to share Jesus with? She tried to calm herself with a sip of tea, but being more flustered than Beth apparently was, she burned her tongue.

She touched her finger to the tip of her tongue instinctively. It stung. "I think that we should talk about Jesus with anyone who is interested. Habiib is interested."

"The timing isn't right, Mia."

Why did Beth always seem so confident?

"What do you mean?"

"I mean, if you push it with Habiib right now, it could endanger our long-term work here."

"So you think that we should withhold salvation from Habiib because it's not convenient for us?" Mia's frustration grew and she felt her face flush. Tzega was sweeping the entryway now, and definitely could hear Mia's tone, even if she didn't understand all the words. But Mia didn't care.

"It's not about convenience, Mia. It's about wisdom. Look, I gotta go. I need to run by the office. I left a couple of Bibles at my desk, and I'd like to get them out of there in case the police come back."

"Wouldn't want them to see that you are a Christian," Mia mumbled.

"What?"

"Nothing," Mia replied. Beth was her only close Christian friend, she didn't want to lose her over a disagreement or ill-thought-out words. "Are we still on for taking the kids to the park tomorrow night?"

"Yes, of course. It'll be fun. Thanks for the tea, Mia. I had a good time. Hey, and you should mention to Michael what I said about Habiib. By the way, I am not coming to church this week. With suspicions so high at the office, I think it is better to lay low."

Mia walked her friend to the gate to wave good-bye as Beth hopped into her SUV and bounced down the bumpy street. The good-bye felt like more than a see-you-later. It felt like a parting of ways.

⇒ Chapter 16 ⇐

The next day, Mia was not in the mood to go to the park with Beth. On the other hand, maybe it would be a good time for them to talk. Maybe she had misunderstood Beth's intentions. When she told Michael about their conversation over tea, he had said as much. Beth was her best friend, after all. She should give her the benefit of the doubt.

It was a school night. Not the best night to be going to the park. But Beth and Mia had determined their park outing would be a great way to meet Sudanese ladies. Most Sudanese social life took place after dark, and if they were going to get to know the locals, they were going to have to adapt their schedules.

Michael agreed to keep Dylan at home so he could go to bed on time. Mia was grateful. Chasing Dylan around the park was not her idea of a good way to meet people. Mia and Beth packed a thermos of hot tea, cookies, teacups, milk, and sugar into a plastic picnic basket and piled into Beth's car with Corey and Annie.

When they arrived at the park, they found a small grassy spot near a set of swings and a metal slide. They spread out a woven mat while the kids ran to the play equipment.

"Don't go far," Mia called after them. She set the basket on the mat and proceeded to pull out the cups and snacks.

Beth groaned as she sat down and stretched her legs out in front of her. "It's so hard to sit on the ground in a long skirt."

Mia laughed. "I know. Here we are wearing long dresses and drinking hot tea. This is definitely *not* how I do picnics in Texas."

"Hey, but at least the kids have playground equipment to play on."

"Have you looked at it?" Mia gestured toward the children. "The swings look like they were made about a hundred years ago, and that slide is so far off of any safety standards ever made for children's playground equipment. I mean look at it, it must be at an 85-degree angle, and there is no lip on the sides. The kids could fly right off."

Beth laughed. "You have a point there. At least your kids are used to stuff like that by now."

"At least Dylan's not here. He'd definitely break an arm."

The ladies settled on the mat and poured cups of tea. Mia had packed a few extra cups in case they found someone to invite to join them. Sudanese always brought plenty of extra food to share with others, so the two had also packed extra cookies.

Mia sipped her tea and looked around the park. Not too far away she saw a group of ladies and children spreading out a mat. The children immediately ran to the swings just as Mia's own children had done. She smiled. Children were the same around the world.

Mia nodded toward the new arrivals. "Maybe we could invite those ladies to come have some tea."

Beth turned to see where Mia was looking. "Great, let's do it. No, wait, looks like some of them are getting ready to pray. We'll have to wait."

Two of the ladies picked up prayer mats and headed to a cemented wash area designated for *wudhu*, prayer washing. The other lady was distracted with a toddler who didn't want to stay on the picnic mat. As she leaned over to grab the arm of the little boy she glanced up and caught Mia's eye. They smiled at each other. Mia understood. Motherhood crossed cultural boundaries too.

"It wasn't long ago Dylan was that age," Mia said.

"You're right. I bet you still remember those days."

"Oh, I do." Mia took a sip of tea. "Maybe I should have brought Dylan tonight. One late night wouldn't have hurt him."

"You told me you'd regret it tomorrow if you did." Beth reminded her.

"You're right, I did. And I would regret it. Dylan needs his sleep. I just hate that I can't get our family schedule to match the Sudanese families' schedule. I can't make late nights work for us."

"I guess that is an advantage to being single," Beth said. "I can set whatever schedule I want. But you're very blessed, you know. At least you have someone to go home to."

Beth was right. Mia battled jealousy over Beth's free schedule and time she spent with Sudanese, but singleness had challenges too. No matter where they lived or what happened during the day, Mia always had Michael to go home to. Beth only had a cat waiting for her at home.

"Look, the ladies are almost done," Beth said.

The two ladies finished their prayers. They picked up their mats, but one of them turned and dropped hers on the ground. It fell and unrolled in a slightly different direction than it had previously been. Mia noticed, but didn't think much of it. When the two returned to their picnic mat, the mother of the toddler took her turn to wash and pray.

Beth caught the eye of one of the women, the younger of the two. Mia thought that she was probably unmarried since she was not wearing the traditional *tobe*, a long cloth that covered the whole body. Instead, she wore a scarf over her hair that coordinated with her denim skirt and long-sleeved purple blouse. Mia used to think it was so strange for Sudanese to dress up for something like a picnic in the park. But now she understood that it was a special outing, just like Mia and Michael might go to dinner or a movie.

"*Utfudulu*," Beth called out, holding their thermos of tea in one hand and the container of cookies in the other.

The women smiled, then looked at each other as if to say, "Should we go over there?"

The older woman pulled the toddler into her lap and motioned for the younger woman to go. She hopped up eagerly and approached Beth and Mia.

"Hello," she said, smiling and holding out her hand to shake.

"I'm Beth and this is my friend Mia."

"I'm Lubna," said the young woman.

"Is that your family?" Beth asked as she motioned toward the picnic mat.

"Yes, that's my mother," said Lubna. "And that is my sister." Lubna pointed toward the woman praying, and she gave a little gasp. She rattled a string of words in Arabic that Mia didn't understand and then excused herself and ran to her sister who was in the middle of prayer.

Beth and Mia looked at each other in confusion. Lubna stopped her sister in midprayer and pointed to the mat. Her sister readjusted the mat to a new direction and began her ablutions from the beginning. Mia noticed the mat was now back to its original position. She resisted the urge to giggle at such a tiny detail.

Then her heart hurt. Did Muslims truly believe Allah wouldn't hear them if the mat was facing a little bit of a different angle? If that was the case, what else had to be exactly right to be accepted by Allah? Mia already knew that Muslim women could not pray during their monthly period. Halimah told her so when she was living with them. They also could not pray during the time that they were bleeding after giving birth.

Lubna returned to Beth and Mia and without explanation sat down again. Beth reached for a teacup to pour a drink for her.

"Oh, no *shukran*," Lubna said. "I will drink tea with my mother."

"Then you must have a cookie," said Beth. "And take some for your family." She grabbed the container and unloaded about half the cookies onto a plate and handed them to Lubna.

Beth was impressive. She had truly taken on Arabic hospitality. Mia would have calculated how many cookies were enough for her own children first before giving any to these acquaintances. She made a mental note to be more generous in the future. Arabs were always so generous, and it was a trait she could definitely improve on.

Lubna took a cookie off the top of the plate and ate it. "It's very good, *shukran*." Just then the toddler began to cry, and Lubna glanced over at her mother. "Oh, I better help her."

"Don't forget the cookies," Beth said, handing her the plate as she stood to leave.

Just then Corey and Annie came running up. Annie stared at Lubna, or rather at the plate in Lubna's hands. "Where are the cookies?" she asked.

"Don't worry, we still have plenty." Mia opened the container and held it up for the kids. Annie grabbed two, as did Corey. Then Corey looked back at the kids on the swings. "I should give some to them," he said.

"Sure," Mia hesitated, then handed him the container. Though they didn't have many left, it would seem strange for her to tell her own son not to share. Corey took it and ran toward the swings. Before he even arrived, the children ran to meet him. They did not devour the cookies as she expected. Each of the children stopped and politely waited for Corey to offer one to them.

Wow, not only can I learn hospitality from Arabs, my kids can learn manners from them.

Corey returned with an empty container.

"Mom, Corey gave all the cookies away." Annie whined as she looked in the picnic basket for more snacks. There were none. She plopped into Beth's lap and frowned.

Beth gave the little girl a hug. "Yes, but look, Annie." She gestured toward the children, who were now returning to the women on the nearby picnic mat. "Look how happy they are." They looked across to where the group was smiling and chattering as they pulled out their own picnic supplies. A few minutes later the children called Corey and Annie over to their mat.

"Go ahead, kids. Looks like they want you to join them."

Corey and Annie jumped up and ran to join the Sudanese group. The young mother had returned from her prayers by now, and all three ladies doted over Corey and Annie.

Beth laughed. "I'm sure they'll have more than their fill of cookies and snacks now."

"And sugar," Mia added. "Just what they need right before bed."

"I love going places with your kids, Mia. They always open doors for meeting new people. When I go out alone, it is not very natural for me to just walk up and meet a Sudanese lady. But with kids, well, it just happens naturally."

"I guess you're right. Most of the people I know here I met through my kids. Except for Abbas and Widad, of course. Hey, that reminds me." Mia launched into a question that had been nagging her the past few days. "You had a copy of the New Testament with you that first time we met Abbas. You gave it to him without hesitating. Why are you now saying we should not be so bold in sharing?"

Beth looked around as if worried they were being listened to. "I just think we need to be more careful. It probably was a bad idea to give him that New Testament before I knew if he was even interested."

"But that's just it. If you felt like you should give it to him, it was probably a prompting from the Holy Spirit. If we feel like we should do something bold, shouldn't we trust the Lord to take care of us? Shouldn't we trust that He is sovereign over anything that could happen to us?"

"Sure, He will take care of us. But that doesn't mean we should do anything stupid."

"Giving a Bible away is never stupid, Beth. That's what I'm trying to say." Mia's voice was strained even though she was trying to keep calm. Why was Beth suddenly so worried about being safe? She hated the tension between them.

"OK, it wasn't stupid," Beth conceded. "We can see that in Abbas's case, it was a good thing. Abbas is actually reading it."

Mia poured another cup of tea and willed herself to change the subject. But she couldn't ask about work. That would bring up the whole Kellar Hope problem, which would end up with Beth's advice to Michael to quit sharing about Jesus at the office. Wasn't there anything else to talk about?

"This is good tea." It was a reach, but all she could come up with. "Did you put cinnamon in it?"

"Yes, I boiled cinnamon and cardamom pods in the water."

"That's what Halimah used to do." Mia missed Halimah. Now, there was a woman who was willing to take a risk for her beliefs.

"Looks like the kids are settling in with their new friends. Let's go talk to Lubna and meet the other two ladies."

"Good idea." Mia set her tea on the mat and stood up. It was tricky to stand up after sitting on the ground in a long skirt, but the longer she lived in Sudan the more adept she got at maneuvering in long dresses and long sleeves.

The two friends walked to the picnic mat and were eagerly greeted by Lubna and her mother and sister. The children were Lubna's five nieces and nephews. They hovered around some trading cards spread out on the mat. Mia smiled. Corey and Annie were right in the mix.

Corey blended in a little bit because of his dark hair but Annie's blond curls glowed in the darkening sky. Mia was proud to see her children adapting so well.

Lubna stood to welcome them. Though the other two older ladies remained seated, they smiled profusely and eagerly shook hands. Within minutes they were seated and eating *sambosas* and sipping hibiscus tea. A cold version of the drink was offered to the kids.

"It tastes almost like fruit punch," Corey told Mia.

The ladies, Mia and Beth learned, were from Omdurman, about half an hour away. The grandfather had dropped them off at the park and would join them later in the evening. The ladies were impressed that Beth and Mia could speak Arabic.

Beth easily turned the conversation to spiritual things. *How does she do that so naturally?*

But even as they chatted, Mia noticed that Beth talked about faith in Jesus as something she personally believed in. She didn't ask the ladies what they thought about it, or if they wanted to know more about Jesus. Should she jump in and ask them what they knew about Jesus? No, at this point in her and Beth's friendship, she didn't want to rock the boat any more than she and Michael already had.

⇒ Chapter 17 ⇐

After helping Corey and Annie get bathed and in bed, the last thing Mia wanted to do was sit at the computer and talk to her mom. It wasn't that she didn't want to talk to her, it was just that she was so tired, and she just wanted to curl up in bed with Michael and go to sleep and not think about the fact that her dad was in the hospital. But it was ten o'clock at night in Khartoum, which mean it was two in the afternoon back in Texas. That was the perfect time for her mom to call because she had probably come home to rest before going back to sit with her dad.

Mia managed to shower before she heard the ring of her mom's call. At least she didn't feel sweaty and dusty from the park anymore. She patted her hair dry with a towel, then grabbed her laptop and headed for the couch in the living room. As she walked, she clicked the *answer* button.

"Hi, Mom."

"Hello? Mia? Can you hear me?"

"Yes, Mom, I can hear you."

"Oh, good, maybe the Internet reception will be good this time."

"I hope so. Sorry we got cut off last time." Actually, Mia wasn't sorry at all. They had gotten into a discussion about safety last time, and her mother was convinced that Mia and Michael did not see the imminent danger that loomed over them and would strike at any moment. Mia had been very thankful that the Internet connection was bad that day. Since then, she had said that Mia should not come home because of her dad, but Mia knew her mother would rather the whole family come home for good.

"You'll be happy to know that Dad will be coming home from the hospital tomorrow. Looks like his stroke was mild and mostly just a scare. He'll be just fine, don't you worry."

"I am so glad to hear that, Mom. Please tell him I am praying every day for him and that I wish I could be there."

"I will, dear. How are Michael and the kids?"

"They are doing fine."

"So is Michael still planning to renew his contract? Or do you think maybe y'all could consider coming on back home?"

Great. We're just going to jump right back into this conversation.

Should Mia tell her mother about the possibility that there would be no contract to sign at all? No. Better not to raise her hopes.

"Yes, we are still planning to sign a new contract. Michael hopes to do that this week."

There was a pause. Then a sigh.

"Well, I guess your dad and I just hoped that two years would get it out of your system."

Mia glanced over at Michael who sat on the other end of the couch grinning at her. He was out of camera view, and she envied him. She wanted to roll her eyes, but her mother had put up with enough eye rolling during Mia's teenage years. No need to regress.

"Well, I don't know when it will get out of our system, Mom. I guess not for another two years."

"I guess so. We won't recognize the children when you come back."

"We were there last Christmas, Mom. We spent our whole three-week vacation with you."

"Yes, but that really wasn't long enough to get to know our grand-kids again."

"You could come here." Mia glanced at Michael who was no longer grinning.

"No way," He mouthed to her. "It's too dangerous for them."

What? Now he was joining her parents in calling Khartoum a danger-ous place. What was it with everyone? It wasn't that bad.

"I don't think Dad would ever do that," her mother said. "He signed up with the US Embassy in Sudan to receive their alert emails. He says there is a travel ban to Sudan."

"Not a travel *ban*, Mom. It's more of advice, a suggestion really."

"You sound like a frog, Mia."

"A frog? Do I sound like I have a cold? I'm fine really. Must be the Internet connection again."

"Not your voice. Your attitude. You sound like a frog in a pot of water. It's getting hot all around you, but you don't notice it."

Here we go again.

"Khartoum is really a pretty safe city, Mom."

"Just be careful, Mia."

"I will, Mom. I love you."

⁂

After hanging up, Mia checked her email. She'd received two from Halimah, though they were written under her new name: Sara. She opened the first one.

My Sister Mia,

I hope you are well. I am doing well. Can you see my English is improving? This is because I have a new job at a refugee center where I am a translator. I am happy in Jesus, but sometimes my life is still very hard. I miss my family so much. Because I am Arab, many people here in Kenya do not trust me. And as for me, it is very hard for me to be friends with them too. I know now that I was raised to be very prejudice. I know that Jesus wants me to love all people. Mia, that is very hard for me. Please pray. I am thinking a lot about my sister Rania. I am praying for her every day. I have asked God if it is OK if I try to contact her. I think He wants me to.

I know you will think this is dangerous, but I called a college friend of mine in Khartoum because I wanted to know how Rania is. Don't worry, I called from a public phone so I did not give away my location. My friend did not have any news for me, but she told me that she saw Rania's name on a list to enter an art contest at some sort of cultural club. I want to give Rania my phone number, but I need your help. I will send you an email with instructions.

God bless you.
Sara

Mia stared at the screen, wrapping a curl of hair around her finger. Was this a good idea? She closed the email and returned to the inbox. There, under the email she'd just read, was the second one. The subject line said "Instructions." Mia braced herself and clicked to open it.

〜〜〜

"Can't you just go visit Abbas by yourself this time, Michael?"

"He insisted that both he and Widad wanted to talk to us. I think you need to come."

"But it's the middle of the week, and I already let Corey and Annie stay up late one night this week when we went to the park."

Michael looked up from the English version of an Arabic newspaper. "I think you'll want to be there, babe. I think Abbas might have been reading the New Testament with Widad."

"Really? I didn't get the feeling she was very interested."

"I know." Michael held the paper as if he were perusing the news on any normal day, but the jitter in his voice belied the excitement.

Mia suddenly didn't care anymore that it might be another late night. They would just have to make it work. Maybe the kids could take a small nap after school, and then they could drive to Abbas and Widad's house.

〜〜〜

"We believe."

Mia couldn't believe her ears. Had she misunderstood the Arabic? Michael and Mia sat with Abbas and Widad in their back courtyard. The kids were playing with Yusra and the other neighborhood kids on the street, probably chasing a goat or kicking a worn out soccer ball.

"We finished reading the whole *Injil* your friend gave us, and we believe all of it. We believe Jesus is the way to God," Abbas said.

"Did you read about Jesus' Crucifixion?" Michael asked.

"Yes, we did. Muslims believe that when Jesus was nailed to the Cross, another person, perhaps Judas, was put there in His place. But Widad and I know now that what we used to believe is not true. We know Jesus was on the Cross."

Michael leaned forward in his chair. "Abbas, there is nothing you can do on your own to have your sins forgiven. All the good works you could ever do will never be enough because God is holy."

"Yes, I know. I've tried for so many years. But when I read this book," Abbas held up the now worn New Testament as tears filled his eyes, "I see there is hope."

"We want to know." Widad leaned forward and looked at Mia quizzically. "When should we be baptized?"

Whoa. Baptized? Mia's heart beat wildly in her chest. She looked across the table at the Sudanese couple. Was this really happening? Could Sudanese Arabs really believe? Sure, Halimah had, but that was before Mia met her. This couple was believing right before her very eyes.

"But why wouldn't they? It's the truth, Mia," Michael said to her as they drove home two hours later.

"It's just that we pray and pray, but I forget that God may actually do what we ask." Mia couldn't stop grinning. She turned to look at Michael as he maneuvered the SUV around potholes and down the dusty streets toward home. He was focused and alert, as a driver always had to be in Khartoum, but he was grinning too. Maybe this was a good time to bring up Halimah. "You know, I got an email from Halimah yesterday."

"How is she?"

"She's good. Got a new job. Her English is improving. She wants to contact her sister and needs my help. Her sister is supposed to be at a concert, and I am to give her Halimah's number. Do you think it's too dangerous?"

"For whom?"

Mia twisted a curl around her finger. "I don't know. It just seems strange."

Michael smiled. "Mia, our whole life got strange when we moved to Sudan. I think it's OK. Halimah would never put you in danger. If she thinks it's OK, you ought to do it. How will you find her sister?"

"Halimah says she'll be at the Jadeed Cultural Center for a concert Friday night. She told me who to find. She said not to stay long because it wouldn't be good for her sister to be seen talking to me. Her family doesn't know any Americans, so it might raise questions. She said if I was quick, no one would notice."

"Well, I guess you better be quick then."

<hr/>

"Are you glad you moved back from Dubai?" Mia asked. She was watching her neighbor Hanaan pour what looked like pancake batter into a pan of boiling water.

"Most of the time, yes." Hanaan stirred the mixture with a wooden spoon. Didi, who always seemed to anticipate her every need, scurried to her side and whisked the empty batter bowl over to the sink and washed it. "I am happy because Sudanese life is slower than life in Dubai. Our family has more time together. I'm happy because our sons can learn about their home culture. Allah has blessed us."

"What about the times you are not glad?"

"Well." Hanaan laughed. "As you know, life in Sudan is very hard. I miss the malls and the easy life in Dubai. If I didn't have Didi here to help me, it would be much harder."

Mia glanced at Didi. The young woman's face did not betray any feelings. She continued to wash dishes. That was the closest Mia had ever heard Hanaan come to complimenting Didi.

Hanaan turned to look at Mia. "And what about you, my friend? Are you glad you came to Sudan?"

"I am." Mia would not have always been that quick to answer in the affirmative. But this time she meant it. She really was glad that her family was here. "I agree that it is very hard though. I am so thankful for Tzega who helps me around the house. Just like Didi, she makes things easier for me."

"Didi, come finish stirring the *aseeda*. But don't burn it. When you are finished, Mia and I will take tea on the veranda."

Hanaan wiped her hands on a kitchen towel and then held up a plastic bowl that looked like a bundt-shaped pan. "When the *aseeda* is as thick as porridge, you pour it into this bowl to cool. Then you turn it upside-down onto a platter and the *aseeda* is finished." She grinned at

Mia. "Simple, right? Now, let's sit outside where there is a breeze."

Before long the ladies were enjoying cups of hot tea and a slight breeze, helped along by a ceiling fan on the veranda.

"My husband said he sees Michael running almost every morning when he is walking to the mosque to pray."

"Yes, he has begun to run for exercise."

"That's very good." Hanaan sipped her tea. "He should be careful though."

"Why is that?"

"Not every Muslim is a good Muslim."

Mia's brow wrinkled. "What do you mean?"

Hanaan reached over and patted her hand. "My family loves your family. We do not have a problem with you, and we know that American politics is separate from American people. Not everyone understands that though. Even the *sheikh* at our mosque does not think highly of Americans. He thinks all Americans agree with everything your government does."

"Is that why I can hear him on the loud speakers on Fridays saying something about *'Amreeka'*?"

Hanaan nodded. "My husband would prefer to pray at a different mosque, but this one is close by and most convenient. You just need to tell Michael to be careful. That's all. Don't worry, Mia. *Insha' Allah* nothing will happen."

Insha' Allah? That was not comforting at all.

"Besides," Hanaan continued, "those who want to hurt others are not true Muslims. Our prophet, peace be on him, taught peace and love. Islam is a peaceful religion. We love people. Even Christians."

That's not what was printed in the news about Sudanese Arabs. But then again, did she want to be like the people Hanaan just mentioned— people who believed a whole group of citizens was just like their government? Of course not. Take Hanaan for example. She was a wonderful person. She was Sudanese Arab and Muslim, yet she was nothing like the terrorists who made the headlines.

Mia remained silent. She disagreed with Hanaan. She did not believe

Islam was a religion of peace. But Hanaan loved Islam so much. Mia did not want to offend her. Besides, it was time to go home.

"Hanaan, this has been a wonderful visit. Thank you for letting me come and watch you make *aseeda*. I need to go home before Dylan wakes up from his nap. It's almost time for Tzega to go home."

"Of course, you are welcome any time."

Hanaan walked Mia to the front gate. Mia kissed both of her friend's cheeks. "*Shukran*, Hanaan."

"*Allah yabarak feekee*," Hanaan replied. She smiled and waved good-bye as Mia walked back to her own house.

As she entered the gate, she was surprised to see Michael's car parked. What was he doing home from work so early? The kids weren't even out of school yet. She walked into the house and found Michael sitting at the dining room table.

"Hi, honey, you're home early."

Michael looked up from his laptop. "Yes, I wanted to show you something."

"Is Tzega still here?" Mia peered into the kitchen before sitting at the table next to Michael.

"No, I told her she could go home early. Dylan is still napping."

Michael leaned down to his briefcase on the floor and pulled out a sheet of paper. He handed it to Mia. It was handwritten in Arabic script. Mia could not understand it, but she did see at the top of the page that the heading read, "Report #5." Mia looked at Michael, trying to decipher from his expression what the paper said. His brow furrowed, did he expect her to be able to read it? Finally he spoke.

"It's a report that was turned in to the police."

"A report like from a spy?"

"Sort of. Yes."

"A report on Kellar Hope?"

"No," Michael replied. "A report on you and me."

W hat do you mean a report on us?"

"Well," Michael took the paper from Mia. "I had Beth look at it because she can read Arabic better than we can." He pointed to the top of the page. "Here at the top it talks about a conversation I had in the office. But it was with only one person, and I know for a fact we were the only ones in the room."

"Who was it? Do I know him?"

"It was Magid. He works on translating documents. He asked me about churches in America. It wasn't a big deal, really. We just talked a short time about it, and I told him that we attend a church here. He asked where it was and when services were held. Then I asked him about praying at the mosque and how often he went and stuff like that."

"It's all in the report?"

"No, just the part about the church we attend. But I don't see how that can hurt anything."

Mia breathed a sigh of relief. It's not like it was a secret that the international community met on Sundays. Nothing that Michael shared was secret information.

"That's not the part that concerns me." Michael ran his finger down to the bottom of the page. "This is our address. It even says, 'wife and three children' right here."

Mia's heart raced, but she set her face in a calm smile. "That's nothing. It's not a secret that you have a family. Nothing you said can get us in trouble."

Michael's face tightened. "Then why file a report on us? And this says it's the fifth report. What do the previous reports say?"

Mia took the paper from Michael and put it down on the table. Then she grabbed his hands. "It doesn't matter, Michael. The fact is we've done nothing wrong. We are here working legally, just like every other person at Kellar Hope. We have to trust that the truth will come out in the end."

"Truth doesn't hold any weight here, babe. This man, whether it's Magid or someone who was listening in, wants something. Either that or the police are bribing him to spy on us."

"Do you think it's Magid?"

"I honestly don't know." Michael squeezed her hand. "It's one thing for me to live in a place like this. But now I've dragged you and the kids here. Look at us, we are being watched. I'm worried about you and Corey, Annie, and Dylan."

"We made this decision together. We decided to move here two years ago, and now we've decided to stay longer. We did that, Michael—you and me. We know this is where we are supposed to be. I'm not worried. God's got this."

"You are so strong, Mia."

"Not really. You are the one who goes out and battles the language and the heat and the culture all day. I stay home mostly."

"But you are my strength." Michael rose from his chair and pulled Mia into an embrace. "I love you."

"We're going to get through this, honey. We won't be bullied by the government or anyone else. Let's just leave this in God's hands and see what He will do."

Mia spoke with confidence, but a catch in her heart reminded her that they were just words. Would she feel as strong if her words were tested?

⁂

That night Mia tossed and turned until she finally fell into a peaceful sleep in the early morning hours. She didn't hear Michael leave at five o'clock for his morning run, but by six she was turning on the coffee maker and waiting for his return. He was later than usual. He always came home in time to shower before they read the Bible together. Mia used the extra time to slip into the shower first, and by the time she got out the coffee was ready to pour.

Awake from her shower, Mia decided to move their Bibles and coffee to the veranda. It was somewhat cool and almost comfortable in such early morning hours. A soft breeze rustled in the lime tree across the yard and the sun was just lighting up the sky to a soft glow.

Mia set two mugs of coffee on the plastic table. *No wonder Michael enjoys running in the morning. It really is quite pleasant.*

She opened her Bible to Acts, deciding to reread the fourth chapter while she waited. When she got to verse three her throat went dry. She read the words aloud.

"They seized Peter and John, and because it was evening, they put them in jail until the next day."

Mia stared at the words. *What if Michael has been seized? What if the police have been waiting outside to arrest him? This would be the perfect time to do it.*

She sat frozen to her chair. Every muscle tensed. Her palms felt sweaty. Whatever strength she voiced the day before now vanished.

They seized Peter and John. They seized . . . Michael.

Mia looked at her watch. 6:15. He'd never been that late before. Maybe he lost track of time. Maybe he miscalculated the distance. She tried to read on but they were just jumbled words. All she could remember was that *they seized Peter and John.*

Fear had a taste. It rolled into her mouth like bile. She felt dizzy. What would she do if Michael were arrested? Who was she supposed to call? Could she tell Hanaan? Was there anyone to help her? She wasn't ready for this. She wasn't strong enough to do this on her own.

Oh, Lord, Michael may be arrested in a foreign country. What do I do? Tears stung her eyes.

She heard a creak and jumped, knocking her coffee to the tile veranda with a crash. The gate opened and a sweaty Michael walked in, calmly shutting the gate behind him.

"Michael, you are late." Mia started to cry.

"Yeah, sorry about that." Michael walked up the steps to the veranda and saw Mia's tears and the broken mug. "What's wrong?"

"Michael, you are late." She repeated.

"Sorry," he said, sounding like a guilty teenager. "I ran into Hanaan's husband on his way home from the mosque, so we talked a little bit out on the road. Where did you think I was?"

Mia was furious—and relieved. "I thought you were . . . you were . . . seized."

"Seized?" The man had never looked more confused.

"Seized!" Mia jabbed her finger at verse three in her open Bible over and over again. As she did, her anger washed away. Relief took over and tears ran freely down her cheeks.

⚜

"Why aren't you running today?" Mia asked Michael the next morning.

"Because we need time to settle this in our minds."

They sat on the veranda with fresh cups of coffee and their Bibles.

"We've been reading in Acts how Jesus' followers spoke boldly about their beliefs, right?"

Mia nodded her head. "But now we are getting into the persecution part. This is a little too close to home, Michael. Maybe we should read a different part of the Bible."

"But that's exactly it, Mia. This is the pattern. We saw it in Halimah's life when she was bold. Persecution comes, but then the good news spreads. That's the equation."

"Are you ready for that?" Mia looked at her husband and saw fire in his eyes. He looked excited and determined all at once.

"More than ever. God is going to walk with us through anything. Just like He did with Halimah when her family beat her for believing in Jesus." Michael set his coffee cup on the plastic table and gently took Mia's hand. "What do you believe?"

When had Michael become such a strong leader? When had his passion for Jesus grown to take over his emotions and actions the way it had in recent days? Mia was proud to be his wife. She wanted to be strong like him.

"I believe the Bible is good news. I believe it's for everyone. I believe God brought us here to Sudan . . ." Mia looked at her open Bible sitting on the table. The pages flipped in the morning breeze—pages filled with stories of people who believed in God and trusted Him with the results, no matter the cost. She looked at Michael, who was staring intently into her eyes, waiting for an answer as if it would determine their next move. "And I believe that God is in control."

They were still words, but Mia was tired of being afraid. It was time to trust God, no matter what.

⁓ₓₓₓ⁓

Michael, Corey, and Annie smiled and waved as they headed off to school and work. Dylan and Mia returned inside to clean up the breakfast dishes.

"Let's play a game, Mommy," Dylan said, as he dried the last plate with a kitchen towel. Mia took the plastic plate from his chubby hand and redried it, placing it in the cabinet.

"OK, I'll tell you what. Let's play a game of my choice first, and then we'll play any game you want to play."

"OK."

"We are going to play 'find the Bibles.' Mommy and Daddy have a lot of Bibles around the house. Can you help find them? It's like a treasure hunt. We'll find all the Bibles and put them in Mommy and Daddy's closet."

"Why?"

"Well, we just think that's a better idea. We can still use them. Here, let me show you." Mia led Dylan into the master bedroom and opened the door to the clothes closet. "See, here on the bottom shelf we can still easily get them."

Mia and Dylan walked through the house together, collecting Bibles and any commentary books they could find. *How does one family accumulate so many?* They left a children's Bible in the kids' room and Michael's and Mia's personal Bibles on their bedside tables. In the end, they had collected two Arabic Bibles, three English Bibles, two commentaries, and a book on how to talk to Muslims about Jesus. All of these, they transferred to the closet.

I bet my friends back in Texas never play "hide the Bibles" with their four year olds. Mia smirked. Her friends in Texas never had to concern themselves with a sudden police search. That was an event that Michael and Mia realized was becoming more and more possible. If they were going to continue sharing, they needed to do so wisely. They agreed it would be good to put away any extra Bibles they had. Owning Bibles was not illegal, but getting them out of view might prevent police from finding a way to accuse Kellar Hope.

"It's my turn now. Let's play," Dylan scratched his curly head, "hide-and-seek."

⇒ Chapter 19 ⇐

Plastic chairs filled the street just in front of the Jadeed Cultural Center. A metal-framed stage took over the far end, accompanied by lights and giant black speakers. Rania nearly turned and walked away, but when she saw many other women and teens dressed like Muslims, her shoulders relaxed and her stomach quit tying itself in knots.

Maysoon, on the other hand, had ripped off her headscarf at some point and now sported a silky hairdo. Her *abaya*, the black robe that she wore on the bus, disappeared, and she wore jeans with silver studs down the side seams with a long glittering tunic-style blouse. Even if it covered every inch of her arms and legs, which it basically did, Rania knew Maysoon's father would never approve of such a wild ensemble.

Rania watched her best friend meander around the chairs and groups of people, smiling and greeting several visitors who didn't even look Sudanese. Sure, they were dark-skinned with Arab features, but they carried themselves like people who'd lived in Europe or the United States.

She clenched her plastic portfolio against her side with her left hand and adjusted her scarf more securely around her face with her right.

A moment later, Maysoon appeared in front of her and smiled brightly. "OK, it's time to show the world your work. Come on." She grabbed Rania's hand, and the girls made their way up the front stairs of an old cement British-style home that housed the cultural center.

The setting sun began to draw the sky into a bluish-brown dust-filled backdrop, and the tiny lights on the bushes surrounding the old house began to twinkle. Rania noticed a green metal sign with letters stenciled in white. "Jadeed Cultural Center: Where the World of Culture Meets Community."

Standing at the top of the freshly mopped steps stood a regal-looking woman in a silk *tobe*. Her tall stature and broad shoulders reminded Rania of Mama, but without the extra weight. Her presence and confidence commanded respect, and Rania felt mesmerized by her green eyes.

"Rania, this is Mel," Maysoon said as they approached the lady.

The younger generation always addressed Rania's own mother as *Um Abdu*. "Mother of Abdu" gave her status, respect, and identity as part of a family, a community, an honorable segment of society. What was "Mel"? Just a name. A simple name gave this tall, beautiful woman no attachment, no status, no reason for respect. These were Father's words bouncing in her head, of course, because Rania thought the name "Mel" was enchanting and wonderful. Still, she couldn't shake her father's voice from her mind.

Maysoon continued, "Mel, this is Rania, the friend that I told you about. She is the talented artist."

"Rania, it's a pleasure to meet you," Mel's voice flowed smoothly from her bright red lips, and her eyes twinkled. Was she wearing colored contact lenses like the models in the Arab women's magazines? She held out her hand, covered in swirls of henna, and shook Rania's. "Maysoon tells me you have some artwork to enter into our expo. I assume that's what you have with you now?" The lady eyed Rania's portfolio.

"Yes," Rania said quietly. She was completely out of her element. This was the craziest thing she'd ever done in her life. She should probably turn and run away right now—go home to Abdu and Ali and wait for Mama and Father to return from Haboba's house and never venture out again. But somehow, she managed to lift the strap of the plastic case from her shoulder and hand it to the magical lady in front of her. As the lady took the case, Rania felt the life she'd always known slip from her fingers.

"Beautiful," the lady said. "I'll have Chookie display these." She turned and handed the case to a mousy guy who stood behind her grinning at Maysoon. He took the case from Mel and whisked them away. As quickly as he did so, a white man and woman approached Mel and began to speak to her in English. She grinned and excused herself to join the couple.

As the girls walked back down the steps and toward the plastic chairs, Rania whispered to Maysoon. "That guy was creepy, the one who took my artwork."

"Who? Chookie? Oh, he's harmless. He's in my group."

"Your group?"

"My hip-hop group."

"You have guys in your group?"

Maysoon threw her head back and laughed.

Maysoon should not be laughing so loudly in public. She seemed so . . . *loose.* " Just wait and watch us when the show starts. You'll love it."

"What's the name of your group? Will you at least tell me that?"

"Freedom." Maysoon smiled. "Perfect, right?"

"Yep, sounds like your kind of group."

"Here, sit right here." Maysoon stopped in front of a row of plastic chairs five seats back from the stage and just in front of two large speakers stacked on top of each other.

"Seriously? In front of the speakers? I'll go deaf."

"Fine, move toward the middle. But stay in this row, you'll have a great view when the show starts."

Rania made her way to the middle of the row and took a seat. She turned to talk to Maysoon, but her friend was walking away.

"Hey," she called. "Where are you going?"

"I've got to go change for the show. We are the first act."

"I have to sit here by myself?"

"I can ask Chookie to send a friend." Maysoon grinned.

"Ha, you're funny. No thanks."

Maysoon disappeared into the cement house, and Rania fished through her purse for her phone. Perhaps Mama had sent her a message. She pushed a button on the screen, and the panel lit up. Sure enough, there was a text from Mama.

Made it to Medani, alhamdulillah. Haboba doing fine. She sends greetings to you. Will be home tomorrow night.

Rania continued to look at her phone, pretending to read and type messages although there were no other ones in the inbox. She tapped her heel against the dusty ground awkwardly. Why had Maysoon left her here to sit all alone? Maybe she should just quietly get up and slip out. She could probably catch a taxi to take her home. That was not really a safe idea, but it was only just now getting dark. She could make it home before Abdu made it back from prayers at the mosque.

"*Salaam aleykum.*" The voice startled Rania, and she fumbled her phone, nearly dropping it on her tapping foot.

"*Aleykum wassalaam,*" she replied on instinct as she turned to see who had spoken to her.

A petite white lady with very blond curly hair pulled back in a ponytail smiled down at her and then sat down beside her. She held out her hand and as they shook, Rania noticed a young boy standing behind her. He leaned around and held out his hand too. He was white like his mother, but his hair was dark brown.

"*Salaam aleykum,*" he mimicked his mother.

Rania couldn't help herself. She smiled. "*Masha' Allah*, praise Allah, he speaks Arabic. I've never heard a *khawadja* child speak Arabic." *Actually, I've never even talked to a white person before. Why in the world are these people talking to me?*

"Are you Rania?" the white lady asked. A curl had loosened itself from the ponytail, and the white lady curled it around her finger as she spoke. Her accent was strong, but her Arabic was correct.

How does she know my name? Perhaps Maysoon told her about me.

"Yes." Rania quit tapping her foot and shifted uncomfortably. "Are you one of Maysoon's hip-hop friends?"

"Hip-hop?" The lady smiled. "No. I don't know Maysoon." Then she leaned in closely, and Rania could smell her perfume. It was faint, but lovely. Rania absently wondered where she had purchased it. In almost a whisper, the lady continued to talk. "I know Halimah."

This time Rania did drop her phone. It thumped in the dirt at her feet and sent a puff of dust into the air. Rania's throat felt as though it closed, and she couldn't breathe. She stared into this strange woman's blue eyes.

What sort of person has blue eyes? Can she be trusted? How does she know Halimah? My family doesn't know any khawadjas.

Rania's eyes brimmed with the questions that filled her heart. The lady must have understood her confusion. She smiled and patted Rania's knee.

"It's a long story, Rania. But Halimah said I could trust you."

"How did you know I was here?" As she spoke, Rania looked around her. More people were filling the plastic seats and a private conversation was impossible. The noise level rose as teens and adults, Sudanese and foreigners, filled the air with laughter and talk. A Sudanese man, perhaps in his twenties, tested the microphone on the stage, and the crackle of a wire with a short in it broadcast loudly over the giant speakers in front of Rania.

Ignoring the question, the white lady pressed a folded piece of paper into Rania's hand. Instinctively, Rania closed her fingers over it.

"This is Halimah's number."

"Is she alive?"

"Just call the number." With that, the white lady stood and grabbed the hand of her son. Rania watched them pick their way out of the row of plastic chairs and walk down the aisle toward the back. The people filing in to take their seats crowded out her view and just like that, the lady vanished.

Rania had no time to consider the paper in her hand. The young man on stage was giving a welcome and the two seats, once taken by the white lady and her son, were quickly filled. She slipped the paper into her purse and held the bag tightly against her chest. She tried to concentrate on the show.

The young man turned the microphone over to Mel, who gave a short welcome speech in Arabic and then added a few words of greeting in English and German. Then the stage and the giant speakers shook as a hip-hop beat overtook the entire area, thumping so loudly that Rania thought her eardrums would burst.

Rania watched as the hip-hop group strutted down the center aisle and up on the stage. There was Maysoon. She wore the same studded jeans, but had changed to an oversized T-shirt with "Freedom" printed across the front. Over the T-shirt she wore a large plaid collared shirt. She wore bright red sneakers and a snapback ball cap of the same color. The others in the group wore similar clothes with hoodies and baggy jeans slung low on their waists.

The group danced about the stage to the beat of the music. Maysoon and a second girl stood to the side singing into microphones secured on stands. They didn't really dance, but Rania knew that her friend would be locked away if her father ever caught her on stage with a group like that. Chookie and the other three guys in the group were pacing back and forth, and they raised their arms up and down. The guys all held microphones, crammed against their mouths like rappers in the music videos Ali sometimes watched with his friends.

Rania's ears felt assaulted, but for the sake of her friend, she strained to understand the fast-paced words of the song.

It ain't the first time,
I've lost my way.
But I've never felt as lousy as I do today.
To date, I've just followed what other people say.
Couldn't muster up the courage to argue or debate.
About to cremate,
Any hopes of changing my fate.
But I know that that's a mistake.

Chookie and the other guys took turns with the lines, and the girls filled in for emphasis. Rania wondered how many practices it had taken them to get the timing right.

Because it'll take a lot more than that to put my dreams in the ground.
When I look up in the sky, all I see are stars around.
And if they can shine strong and bright, even through the night,
Then as long as the world keeps spinning, I will survive this fight.
No need to ask me twice, I've made up my mind.
I've listened to enough advice, I know what I need to find.
Freedom. Freedom. Freedom.

The music stopped, and the hip-hop group waved enthusiastically before exiting the stage. Rania was impressed by Maysoon's performance. Maybe hip-hop wasn't Rania's thing, but she couldn't deny that Maysoon was pretty good at it.

After a second hip-hop group—who Rania thought weren't nearly as good—a pop group performed, and then Mel announced an intermission and encouraged the audience to look at the artwork displayed inside.

Rania made her way toward the center aisle, searching for Maysoon. She didn't have to look long. Her friend came bounding down the stairs of the cement building, beaming.

"How was it?" she asked, her eyes sparkling like the lights that twinkled on the bushes around the center.

Rania grabbed her friend's hands and squeezed them. "You were amazing."

"Really?"

"Yes, you really were." Rania thought about Maysoon's family. What did it matter if Maysoon was the most amazing hip-hop performer there was? She'd never be allowed to do this again, once her father found out. She considered saying this, but then she saw the hope in Maysoon's eyes that gleamed like those of a star-struck little girl. Maysoon was not ignorant. She knew the truth; Rania needn't remind her.

"We need to get home before my parents wonder where we are. I talked to Mel, and she said she'd let me know how your drawings did in the competition." Maysoon slung her bag over her shoulder. Rania noted that she'd changed back into her long tunic as well as the black *abaya*. There was no sign of her hip-hop clothes. Either she'd left them with someone from her group or crammed them into her bag.

Maysoon's family had a lovely home with air-conditioning units in each bedroom. Even so, the girls slept on metal beds on the flat roof. A cool breeze freshened the night, even though dust filled the air. Rania pulled a sheet up over her head to hide light from the street lamp, and she squeezed her eyes shut. Maysoon already slept soundly—probably dreaming about her performance.

What is Maysoon wanting freedom from anyway? She says she wants to be free from expectations and her strict Muslim culture, but she's only trading one culture for another. Isn't hip-hop culture, or Western culture, just as dictatorial and demanding? She's replacing one set of rules for another. Is that freedom?

Rania thought about the slip of paper in her purse. Was it really Halimah's phone number? The white lady told her to call the number. Rania mustered every ounce of self-control not to call the number now that Maysoon was asleep. Better not risk it. She would wait until she was truly alone.

※※※

Saturday was a day off, so Rania helped Maysoon hand-wash some clothes and hang them on the clothesline in the *hosh*, the open area downstairs. Maysoon's family had a clothes washer, but her mother did not trust the modern machine. "Hand washing is much better," she insisted. "Those machines do not do a very good job."

Maysoon's family enjoyed a close relationship. But they were strict. Both parents participated in the *Haj*, the pilgrimage to Mecca that all Muslims are encouraged to take. Both of Maysoon's older brothers had also been to the holy city in Mecca, and Maysoon was next on the list. Her family planned for her to join her parents in the coming year. Rania had overheard Maysoon's mother telling her own mother all about it. "When Maysoon sees Mecca, she will become more devout. She will learn how beautiful and peaceful Islam is and will want to become much more dedicated to Allah. Perhaps she will become a *munaqiba*."

Maysoon's mother was referring to a woman who covered herself totally, complete with socks, gloves, and a face covering that left only a slit opening for the eyes. Maysoon would never agree to become a *munaqiba*. No, her head was filled with thoughts of freedom and breaking out of what she insisted was a stifling culture.

Thankfully, Maysoon didn't ask Rania what she thought about

freedom. If she had, Rania would have said the answers were in a little book she was reading. The thin book with a blue paper cover and yellow letters on the front held the answers. *Injil Yohana*. For just a moment Rania worried that Abdu had scoured her bedroom while she was gone. Would he do the same to her as he'd done to Halimah if he found her book? What was so important about that book that roused such anger in the men of her family?

If Abdu hasn't found it by the time I get home, I'm going to take it out and read the whole thing.

⁂

Rania returned home Saturday before her parents arrived from Medani. She found her room untouched and was relieved to peek behind the wardrobe and see the purse still wedged in its location. She busied herself cleaning the house and splashing the cement *hosh* with water so the dust wouldn't be swirling around when her parents arrived.

By the time Father and Mama pulled up in their sedan, the house was spotless. Mama unloaded pots of homemade sauces and bags of bread from Medani. "Gifts to you kids from Haboba," she said.

Father and Mama slipped right back into their roles, just as if they had been at home all along. Father called Jamal and invited him to come for tea. Mama busied herself fluttering about the kitchen.

Rania served tea to Father and his guests that night. She was increasingly concerned with what she wore when Jamal visited. And that night, as she stirred sugar into the teacups, she imagined that she and Jamal were married and she was serving Jamal and his guests instead of Father.

Maybe this could work. Maybe we could get married and search for answers together. We could read the book together.

"Rania?"

"Yes, Father?"

"I think the sugar is sufficiently stirred."

Rania wasn't sure how long she'd been kneeling at the coffee table stirring the teacups. She cleared her throat and gave one of the cups a final stir, as if she knew just what she was doing. Then she sat a cup in front of each of the men and excused herself.

Later in the evening Rania returned to the salon where the men had been visiting. Father and two of the men were standing outside, so she assumed that everyone was leaving. Jamal, still sitting in one of the sofas, startled her.

"Oh, I'm sorry. I thought you were gone."

Jamal grinned. "Your father wanted me to stay. He wanted to tell me something."

"Oh?" Rania asked. Perhaps he was going to find out if Jamal was interested in marriage? "What about?"

"I don't know." Jamal leaned forward and gazed at Rania. He glanced toward the door. The loud voices of the men in the *hosh* drifted into the salon. Jamal looked back at Rania and smiled. Rania's heart beat wildly. The men's voices stopped, and Rania heard the metal gate shut. As Father's footsteps neared the front door, Rania quickly gathered the empty teacups on the tray and whisked them away to the kitchen. She didn't turn to look, but she felt sure that Jamal still smiled at her as she left. She was smiling back.

I should call Halimah's number, I could tell her all about Jamal. She would be so happy. What if I call and it's not her? What if it is her, but she doesn't believe the book anymore? I don't know what I would do.

It didn't matter what she thought about the number because she hadn't been alone long enough to call it anyway. Rania tucked her questions away in her mind, like the piece of paper that was tucked away in her purse.

⸎

A week passed before Maysoon brought news of the art expo at the cultural center.

"You won first prize for the picture with all the words on it."

"I did? Are you sure?"

"I'm sure. Mel called and told me. She says you won prize money." Maysoon stopped right in the middle of the street as the girls walked to school. She grabbed Rania's hands and looked into her eyes. "Rania, you are an artist."

Rania smiled. "I am, aren't I?"

"Yes." Maysoon began walking again and Rania followed suit. "You are an artist and you need to study art. I think you should move in with me."

"With you? Your family is so strict, they would never let me study art."

"No, silly. I'm leaving home. You should leave home too."

"Leaving home? I thought you were kidding."

"I'm not. I found a room to rent and I already paid for it."

"Where?"

"A place that Chookie found for me. There are some other girls renting rooms in the same building."

Rania frowned. "Maysoon, girls don't live alone. Not good girls."

"Maybe not in Sudan, Rania, but everywhere else in the world they do. Anyway, 'I've made up my mind. I've listened to enough advice, I know what I need to find.'"

"You're quoting that song your group sang."

"Yes. And I believe in it."

"In what?"

"In freedom."

⇒ Chapter 21 ⇐

The Holy Month of Ramadan arrived with great anticipation. Rania didn't know if the month of fasting would begin on Thursday or Friday. Sudan still held to the tradition that its citizens had to wait for a committee in Saudi Arabia to sight the moon and declare the news to the rest of the Arab World. Finally, the announcement came over Father's crackling radio that the group of Muslim leaders in Saudi Arabia had seen the sliver of a new moon in the sky and, therefore, Ramadan began on Thursday. This meant that, beginning at sunrise Friday morning, all Muslims must fast from eating, drinking, smoking, and even marital relations from dawn to sunset for an entire month.

"This is a time when we draw close to Allah," Father said. "A time to lay aside our human desires and purify our hearts."

The schools in Khartoum were closed for Ramadan, so Rania spent much of her mornings reading the Book of John that Halimah left for her. She finished the whole thing and started again. This strange little book was so different than anything she read before—so different than what she heard the *sheikh* preaching at the mosque on Fridays. *Isa* spoke about loving others and about peace, healing, and hope. Rania especially liked the story of the woman who was going to be stoned. She'd heard of a woman being stoned in a village outside of Khartoum. It was for the same reason as the story in the book. Both women were accused of committing adultery. The woman in the village had died. But in this book, *Isa* rescued the woman.

In another story, *Isa* talked to a woman who was very sinful and told her about "living water" that she could drink that would quench her thirst. That woman was like Maysoon. Maysoon was thirsty—thirsty for freedom. Maysoon thought that moving out of her home and joining a singing group would give her the freedom she wanted. But would it?

On Friday, after the first full week of Ramadan, Rania sat on her bed, her back against the wall, and flipped through the Book of John. She did not hide it behind the wardrobe anymore because it was too hard to retrieve as often as she'd been reading it lately. She now kept it hidden under her mattress.

I should call the number to find out if it is truly Halimah's number. I could tell her all about what I have been learning.

Rania had been awake since four in the morning when she and Mama prepared a meal for the family. Everyone must eat before the call to prayer just before sunrise so they would have strength for a full day of fasting. Sleepy as they were, they ate and drank in haste. Then the *muezzin's* voice drifted through the predawn air, "*As-salatu khayroon minan-nawm*. Prayer is better than sleep."

At that, Father, Abdu, and Ali left to attend prayers at the mosque while Mama and Rania washed the dishes and put away the leftovers. After the kitchen was tidy, Mama returned to her room and went back to sleep. Rania's sleepy body ached to do the same thing, but with the men out of the house, now was the perfect time to read her book. She wouldn't call the number yet. Mama was just one room over and would be able to hear her voice through the thin walls. She ached to talk to Halimah, but the time was not right. She had to be patient.

Rania flipped back to another one of her favorite stories. It was about a man named Lazarus who had died. According to the book, *Isa* had raised him back to life again.

Could this be true? Could *Isa* have raised someone from the dead? If so, he must surely be sent from Allah. The prophet Mohammed had never done anything like that. And then a dangerous thought entered her mind: what if *Isa* was truly sent from Allah and Mohammed was not?

Rania once heard a similar story a long time ago when she was very sick. She was lying in bed with a terrible fever. She remembered the heat she felt on her skin, like she was baking from the inside out. Words and visions fluttered in and out of her mind and she couldn't focus. Noises made her head throb.

Somewhere in the pain and chaos of her mind, she remembered a soft voice, the voice of her sister, Halimah. The smooth tone and the peaceful cadence of the words calmed Rania. She listened to the story of a little girl who had been healed. Rania remembered hoping that she was that little girl. That's all Rania remembered. What was the name of the man who healed the little girl in the story? Rania squeezed her eyes shut and tried to remember.

Yes. Yes, I'm pretty sure it was. I'm pretty sure I remember hearing Halimah say that it was Isa. *It was* Isa *who healed the little girl in the story.*

As Rania recalled the event in her mind, she almost felt Halimah's hand resting on her forehead. She leaned her head against the wall and recalled her sister's voice. *Jesus, if You will heal Rania, then I will believe that You are God.*

Rania's eyes flew open. Yes, she remembered it fully now. It was almost two years ago that she had been racked by a terrible fever. But she remembered now, Halimah had prayed for her and asked *Isa* to heal her. And He had.

⁓⁓⁓⁓⁓⁓

Almost every morning during the month of Ramadan, Rania cooked food with her mother, cleaned up the kitchen, then returned to her room. Almost every morning she imagined calling the number that was in her purse, but somehow she could not gather the courage. So much was riding on who answered the phone. So she read the book. Were there more books about *Isa*? She hoped so. She had no idea how to find out.

What about all those books that Halimah used to have? Rania cringed. It was the large stack of books that caused Halimah to get in trouble.

Rania remembered seeing books in Halimah's wardrobe, but at the time, Rania paid no attention.

Rania remembered the night Abdu came into their room. Halimah was not home, and Rania was reading a magazine on her bed. She remembered Abdu throwing open the bedroom door without so much as a knock. He walked straight over to Halimah's wardrobe and opened the door. Then he began to pull clothes out off the shelves, tossing them on the floor.

Rania was about to fuss at him when she saw him reach both hands into the wardrobe and pull out the stack of books.

She gasped. She hadn't realized Halimah owned so many. She glanced from the stack to Abdu's face. That vein on his forehead bulged. She'd never forget it.

He stomped out of the room and before she had a chance to pick up all of Halimah's clothes from the floor, Mama came to the door and told her to leave.

"Go to Maysoon's house. Now, Rania."

Rania remembered grabbing her magazine and a scarf for her head and rushing out of the house. It was such a strange request because she hardly knew Maysoon back then. But the tone of her mother's voice demanded immediate obedience.

Late that night, when Rania returned home, Father pointed to Halimah and said, "This girl is no longer my daughter, and she is no longer your sister. Rania, you are my only daughter now."

Rania had looked at her battered sister and cried. And even now, as Rania recalled the events of that day, a tear rolled down her cheek. Her hands folded tightly around her little book, her only connection to Halimah.

"*I want you to read it.*" She could hear Halimah's voice. "*It will tell you the truth, Rania. No matter what happens, remember it will tell you the truth.*"

<hr>

"Who is coming to break the fast with us today?" Rania asked her mother.

The two women worked side by side in the kitchen. Rania diced potatoes to cook and mix with other vegetables while Mama shaped meatballs and placed them on a baking sheet.

"A new guest."

Rania eyed her mom. "That sounds vague."

Mama smiled.

"What's that about?" Rania raised her eyebrows. "And anyways, I'm surprised it's not Jamal."

Mama frowned.

Rania stopped cutting potatoes and stared at her mother. "What, Mama?"

"Jamal is engaged."

Rania's stomach lurched. She felt nauseous. *Engaged? Jamal?* "What do you mean?" She squeaked.

Mama sighed. "I mean Jamal is engaged. He's going to marry his cousin."

"I thought . . ."

"Rania, don't worry. Your father is already working on a new plan for you. Make sure you look nice for tonight."

Rania tried not to cry. But a tear betrayed her and made its way down her cheek. She ignored it and forced herself to return to dicing potatoes.

༶༙༙

Later that afternoon, Rania obediently dressed nicely for Father's guest. She helped her mother serve food and clean the kitchen. She did all the things a good daughter should do. But she felt like a robot. Her heart ached. Where was Jamal?

The young man who came as a guest was apparently a distant cousin. Father was thrilled, and even Mama seemed pleased at the connection. He was tall and had a giant smile. He wore the traditional *jallabeeya* and he sported a *zibeeb* on his forehead. A *zibeeb* was the purple bruise on the foreheads of pious men who pressed their foreheads to the ground when they prayed.

Rania screwed up her nose when she first saw it. *There goes my chance to learn more about* Isa *and to study art. A guy with a* zibeeb *is not going to be open to new ideas. What was I thinking anyway? There's no way for a girl like me to escape. I'm stuck. I'll be a good Muslim wife and mother like Haboba, like Mama, like my daughters after me.*

༶༙༙

"But Mama, Ramadan is almost over. Will you be home for *Eid al-Fitr*?"

"I don't know, Rania."

Mama threw some clothes into a small bag while Rania watched from the doorway.

"Can I come?"

"No, Father needs you here to cook for them while I'm away. I

122

wouldn't go if Haboba hadn't asked me to come. She sounded so weak on the phone."

"What is she sick with?"

"I don't know. That's why I need to go. I'll try to be back soon."

With that, Mama was gone. She traveled to Medani with a family from the neighborhood who had planned to spend the upcoming holidays there. Rania didn't remember Haboba ever being sick.

Rania sulked in her room. Mama was gone. Jamal was marrying his cousin. Maysoon had run away from home and lived who knew where with who knew what kind of people. Rania was alone. Should she use the number and try to call Halimah? With Mama out of the house, perhaps she could find a time when she was home alone to finally gather the courage to call. But not now. Ali was in the salon watching television. She would wait for the perfect time, then do it. She would call Halimah.

Rania walked to her room, deciding now would be a good time to draw. She remembered the simple tree she'd once drawn. It was one of her first drawings, and it looked so novice. Rania pulled out a new pack of art paper and her pencils. She began a new drawing of a tree. Her dark mood came out on paper in black and browns and dark greens. The gloomy shades swirled through the branches and the leaves. The tree seemed to strain against an unseen force. Rania's mood lifted as she continued to draw, as if the colors and patterns expressed the bits of her heart that words could not. She lost herself in the project and did not stop until the entire page was filled with colors. When she held her finished work in her hands, she thought perhaps the tree was her best work yet. In spite of the dark colors, the picture was very beautiful.

≫ Chapter 22 ≪

Sudanese Embassy Warden Message: We have received credible information of impending actions against citizens of Western nations residing in Sudan. We advise all American citizens, as always, to be vigilant. Avoid crowded areas, and vary your routes and times of movement around Khartoum."

Oh, that's just great. Mom and Dad get these messages, so they'll see this when they open their email.

Mia prayed her parents wouldn't freak out. It was a simple warning, a reminder from the embassy. Nothing to worry about. In years past, Mia would worry just as much as she imagined her mother was now. But since she and Michael had made their decision not to fear, a sense of peace had overtaken her emotions.

Michael was staying at the office late again, so Mia put the children to bed—another night without the kids saying good night to their dad. She sighed. She didn't blame him. He needed to work hard at the office, especially if someone was watching him.

The reports didn't really worry them. During working hours Michael was as diligent, or more so, than anyone else at the office. How could he be accused of doing anything wrong after work hours? Hours not spent at work were personal, right?

Beth disagreed. She had begun to more frequently warn both Michael and Mia to guard their actions and words even during their free time.

"It's different here, Mia," Beth said. "You don't have rights in Sudan. No one but the president and his cronies have rights. If the law says you can't proselytize, you just can't."

But Mia wasn't really proselytizing. She was just sharing what she believed. People could decide for themselves what they wanted to believe. She wasn't forcing anyone to change. That was their choice. But Mia already knew what Beth's response would be. It wasn't worth arguing with her.

"In Sudan the people don't have choices, Mia. They are born Muslim or Christian. They don't believe it is possible to change."

Mia curled a strand of hair around her finger while dialing Michael's cell number. She'd better tell him about the embassy email.

The house phone clicked a couple of times before Michael answered. That was unusual. Maybe the connection was bad. Michael answered in Arabic. He must not have seen her number appear before he picked it up.

"Hi, honey."

"Hi, sorry I'm late again. I'm just finishing up and then I'll be home."

"It's OK, do what you need to do. I just wanted to tell you we got a warning message from the embassy." The phone clicked again. "Michael, are you there?"

"Yeah, I'm here."

"OK. Well, anyway, it says to be vigilant. And to vary our routes. Maybe you should come home from work a different way."

"OK, I will. You aren't worried are you?"

"No, I'm fine. Really I am. We just need to be careful, that's all."

Mia said good-bye and hung up the phone. She didn't just say those words to sound strong for Michael. She really did believe it.

She began an email to her parents hoping some family news would set their hearts at ease:

Dear Mom and Dad,

Hi from Khartoum! We are doing great. Corey and Annie love their school. I've told you before that they attend an international school that is taught in English. The classes only have five or six students in each grade, which I really like. The teachers, though, are from South Sudan and teach British English. Corey is now using British spelling and Annie insists that cookies are called "biscuits."

Mia paused . . . should she mention the warden message? She decided to end with:

I know you probably received the email from the US Embassy. Please don't let this message worry you. We are fine and we will continue to monitor the situation here. If things ever heat up in Sudan and we feel we are not safe, we will leave.

When Michael returned at ten o'clock, Mia was nodding off on the couch.

"Hello, babe," he said as he bent over and kissed her forehead. "Why didn't you just go on to bed?"

"I can't go to bed while you are still out. I need to know you are safely home. Did you come home a different way?"

Michael looked at her sheepishly. "I forgot. But I'll do that tomorrow."

⁂

The morning Michael came home late from running Mia had been so worried she hadn't read the rest of Acts 4. It was right there in front of her: the answer to her panic attack. She had only been focusing on verse three and the words, "they seized."

"But many who heard the message believed," Mia read it again to herself. Yes, there was persecution in Acts, but the gospel was spread. If Halimah was right, and persecution was the path to the spread of the truth about Jesus in Sudan, Mia had to ask herself if she was willing to take her own path through persecution.

Mia continued to read, starting in verse 12, the words that she and Michael had just read together over coffee.

"'Salvation is found in no one else, for there is no other name under heaven given to mankind by which we must be saved.' When they saw the courage of Peter and John and realized that they were unschooled, ordinary men, they were astonished and they took note that these men had been with Jesus . . . Then they called them in again and commanded them not to speak or teach at all in the name of Jesus. But Peter and John replied, 'Which is right in God's eyes: listen to you, or to him? You be the judges! As for us, we cannot help speaking about what we have seen and heard.'"

A sound at the front gate startled Mia and she left her Bible on the dining table and ran to the front door. It was Tzega arriving for work.

So jumpy . . .

Dylan, who ventured outside while Mia was reading, now walked in holding Tzega's hand and smiling. Perfect timing. Mia needed to go grocery shopping, and with Tzega at the house, she didn't have to drag Dylan along with her.

〜〜〜

Grocery shopping in Khartoum was hunting and gathering of a different kind. There were only two stores in the whole city that carried imported goods. Mia hit those stores first. They were each about the size of a gas station back home, although one was two-story, so about twice the size. She found some canned green beans in one of the stores. They were $3 each, but she grabbed two anyway. Boxed cereal was out of the question. At $8 for a box of an unknown brand of corn flakes, Mia opted for a box of oatmeal instead. Thankfully there was always tomato paste and cheese. Mia could make a variety of meals with those two ingredients.

After the two import stores, Mia went to her usual place to buy vegetables. The open-air stands stood in a line under a row of neem trees. The proprietor of the first vegetable stand was very kind to Mia. He was helpful when she asked about fresh mint or if he had any zucchini. He handed her a plastic bag to fill with potatoes. Her sweaty palms mixed with the dirt that covered the knobby bulbs and formed mud that made the process slippery. A kilo of potatoes, a half kilo of carrots, a small bunch of mint for their tea, and two large onions. The season was too hot for green beans, so Mia was glad she'd paid for canned ones. She handed the money to the man, when he told her the price, and received the change without ever looking him in the eye.

"*Shukran*, thank you."

"*Allah yabarak feekee.*" He replied and promptly, almost rudely, went on to his next customer. Mia was not offended. This was the usual manner for a polite man who respected her.

The men at the fruit stand were a different story. Mia felt dirty around them. And it had nothing to do with the mud on her hands. Two of them leered at her as she approached. She wished she knew a different place to buy fruit. But she steeled her approach and focused on the oranges. As quickly as possible she grabbed one of the plastic bags sitting atop a pyramid of melons and began filling it with the oranges. She'd become fairly accurate at guessing the weight of produce, so she gathered about a kilo and handed it to one of the men to weigh it. She didn't look him in the eye, but could tell he was looking her up and down. It was for just a moment and then a laugh from his friend, and then they reverted back to acting like respectable men. No one else seemed to notice. She wished the vegetable man had seen and would come to her rescue. She hated to give these buffoons any money, but her children needed fruit.

"Anything else, sister?" asked the man who had weighed the oranges for her.

"A kilo of bananas, please."

"Wan KEElow pananasssss," he said loudly in his attempt at English. His friend laughed again and slapped the man on his back. Mia paid the price as quickly as she could and spun around to head back to the safety of her car. As she did she bumped into a small girl. A beggar.

"Oh," She exclaimed, "*Malesh*, excuse me."

The girl was probably nine or ten, about Corey's age. Her dark skin was covered in dust so that it was more grayish brown than black. Her hair, cut short, was filthy. Her eyes were an empty glaze. Her ill-fitting dress hung off one shoulder. Her feet were bare.

Mia looked down at the girl. Long ago, Mia's heart would have broken. But if Mia's heart broke every time she saw poverty or human suffering, she wouldn't have made it for two years in Sudan. She looked down and smiled at the girl. "What is your name?"

"*Fuloos*, money."

"Your name, what is your name?"

The dirty beggar girl raised her eyebrows in surprise. "You speak Arabic."

"Yes," Mia said. "Now, what is your name?" Mia continued walking toward her car because she wanted to get away from the men at the fruit stand.

"Lily," the girl said. For a moment a lucid glint crossed Lily's eyes.

Mia glanced at Lily's left hand. She clutched a gray rag. Paint thinner. The girl sniffed paint thinner to escape her problems. Many of the street kids did. Mia winced. More money would buy her more paint thinner.

"Lily, I can't give you money. I will give you an orange." Mia reached into the plastic bag and pulled out the round fruit.

Lily shook her head. Her eyes glossed over again. "*Fuloos. Fuloos,*" she insisted.

"No *fuloos*, Lily." Mia nudged the orange into Lily's free hand. She reluctantly took it.

Mia opened the car door. As she struggled to get her bags of fruits and vegetables situated in the back seat she felt Lily tapping her with the sniffing rag. She cringed.

"*Fuloos. Fuloos,*" Lily whimpered in a whiny pitiful voice.

What else could Mia do? Give her another orange? The girl didn't even want the one she had. Mia shut the back door and opened the driver door while Lily rubbed her arm with the rag and whined. Mia fought back frustration. What did Lily expect from her? Best to just drive away. Mia pulled the door, but it wouldn't shut.

What in the world?

She tried again but the door wouldn't shut. Then she realized that Lily had flipped the safety latch on her door that kept it from shutting properly. Irritation flooded her veins. Lily had been trained by the older street kids how to get to the *khawadjas*, the expats. Without the ability to shut the door, the beggars had free access to pester the rich driver until they gave money. Mia glared at Lily and reached out to flip the latch back. She shut and locked the door. Lily remained just outside the car, rubbing her sniffing rag on the side window and whining.

Mia's nerves were shattered. She just wanted to get away. She started the car and quickly put it in reverse. As she backed away she heard a bang followed by Lily screaming. She slammed on the brakes and gasped. Against her will she looked out the window in terror at what she might see. She saw Lily crying and grabbing her arm, but there was no blood, and her hand still grasped the orange. Lily pretended to be hit by the car in a final attempt to get money.

Mia had been irked, but now she was just plain mad. She had been nothing but nice to that girl. How could that ungrateful beggar treat her so rudely? Mia scowled and immediately realized she'd hit a new low. She glared out the smudged window at Lily, who took a bite out of the orange without peeling it, as if it were an apple, and stared at Mia.

As she drove away, Mia looked in the rearview mirror just as Lily launched the orange at her car. It went thump on the back windshield and left a sticky splash that dripped slowly down the glass. Mia scowled again. No wonder she'd given up her empathetic feelings and soft heart.

❧ Chapter 23 ❧

Mia was exhausted after grocery shopping. Today was not a great shopping day. But who was she kidding? This was the way it was every time she shopped.

Tzega helped Mia unload the groceries and promptly started washing the produce.

God bless Tzega. What a lifesaver.

Dylan was busy watching a children's show on DVD. Mia smiled. Tzega had no idea how to run a DVD player, which meant that four-year-old Dylan had showed her how to do it.

Mia poured a glass of water, which she promptly gulped down in its entirety. She filled the glass again and set it on the kitchen table while she tried her hand at making *aseeda* batter. After mixing some of her newly purchased sorghum flour with water, she then gently stirred in two large spoonfuls of yogurt, just like Hanaan taught her. The batter would need to ferment for one day, then it would be ready to cook like porridge.

Mia grinned at Tzega. "I am going to try to make *aseeda*. I hope I like it." Tzega wrinkled her nose, which made Mia laugh. "Tzega, I was wondering, where is your hometown?" Mia asked.

"Asmara, in Eritrea."

"And your husband is Ethiopian?"

"Yes."

"Do you miss Asmara?"

"I miss the way it was when I was young," Tzega said. "We were a brand new free country, and our president lived very simply, just like us. We were free to roam the streets and free to believe what we wanted."

Mia looked at Tzega. Her eyes sparkled as she spoke. She continued to wash vegetables under the faucet. A gentle grin settled on her lips.

"It's not like that now?"

"No."

"What happened?"

"Many things," Tzega said. The grin and the sparkle faded. Sadness crept over her face. "Our president changed."

"You got a new one?"

"No, he's the same man. But his heart changed."

"Ahhh," Mia said. "We have a saying in English, but I don't know how to say it in Arabic. 'Absolute power corrupts absolutely.' Sorry, I don't know how to translate that."

"It's OK."

The ladies worked in silence. Tzega had been working for her for several weeks now and Mia didn't know that much about her.

She was relieved to hear Tzega speak again.

"My father is a pastor."

"Really? I didn't know that. What church?"

Tzega said the name, but it was in Tigrinya, the Eritrean language, so Mia didn't understand it. "Protestant," Tzega said.

"And is he pastoring in Asmara?"

"No," Tzega said. "He's in prison."

"I'm sorry, I didn't hear you, did you say *prison*?"

"Yes, it is now illegal to be a member of our church. There are only three churches recognized by the government of Eritrea, and our church is not one of them."

"Can't one of the other churches register for you?"

Tzega shook her head. "They are too scared."

"So . . ." Mia spoke with caution. "Your father?"

"Yes, he is in prison. I don't know where. But he is in Eritrea somewhere. They won't tell my mother anything. We pray that he is in Massawa. At the prison in Massawa, they do not beat the prisoners as badly as the other prisons."

A wave of nausea came over Mia. How could Tzega be so strong? The queasy feeling subsided enough for her to sit at the kitchen table. She grabbed her cup of water and took a sip. What should she say?

"I pray he is too," Mia said, even though her words felt trite.

"This is not America," she heard Beth's words again. *"You left your rights when the airplane's wheels left American soil, Mia."*

Before coming to Sudan, Mia was oblivious to the suffering of people in places like Sudan and Eritrea. And her friends and family still were.

How could she even begin to explain situations like this to them? That's why she wrote fewer emails now.

Mia looked at Tzega. She methodically washed and dried the vegetables and fruits and placed them in the fridge so the heat would not ruin them. She was calm. She was in control of her emotions. How many other terrible things had happened to her? She bore it all with such dignity.

"Should I iron the clothes now?" she asked.

Mia couldn't speak. She simply smiled and nodded. As Tzega left the kitchen, she stopped at the door and turned to look at Mia in the eye. "Thank you for praying for my family, for my father."

"I am honored to," Mia said. And she was.

<hr />

Tzega finished her work and left after washing the lunch dishes. Dylan lay down for his afternoon nap. It was only then that Mia sat on the veranda outside and relaxed a little. She'd been running from one thing to the next all morning—each situation more challenging than the one before. But this—the fact that Tzega's father was in prison somewhere in Eritrea, being beaten for his Christian beliefs—this was too much to bear alone.

She needed to talk to Michael. He was busy at work, she knew, but she needed some perspective. She dialed his number and listened as the phone started to ring, then she shook her head and hung up. No, this was something she needed to deal with on her own. She leaned back in the plastic chair and squeezed her eyes shut. She tried to envision God sitting on His throne looking down at her. But all she could see was a hazy cloud.

God, there is so much that is wrong here. Are You even able to reach down through the haze and intervene on behalf of people in Sudan? What about Eritrea? I know the Bible says You can. Forgive me for feeling this way, but sometimes I doubt it.

Mia recalled a verse from somewhere in the Gospels that said, "Because you have seen me, you have believed; blessed are those who have not seen and yet have believed." She needed that kind of faith.

⇒ Chapter 24 ⇐

At 2:30 Mia started to get agitated with Michael for being late. He always took a late lunch break to bring Corey and Annie home by two o'clock. Maybe he was having car trouble. But then again maybe he had so much on his mind that he'd forgotten.

She dialed his number and let the phone ring. The connection clicked and rang, but Michael didn't answer. *What is up with all the clicking? Why can't they get their phone lines to work?* Mia punched the *end* button in frustration.

She dialed the school office.

"No, Mr. Weston has not come by to pick them up yet. They are sitting in the office with me."

"I'll be there as soon as I can."

Seriously, Michael? You could have at least called me so that I could arrange for someone else to pick them up.

Hanaan was nice enough to send Mia and Dylan with her driver to pick up Corey and Annie. They were sitting side by side on a wooden bench just on the other side of the secretary's desk.

"I'm so sorry, Margaret," Mia said to the Kenyan woman. "I don't know what happened with Michael. He must be in a meeting at work or something."

"Don't worry, madam," Margaret replied. "These things happen."

"Come on, kids, let's go." Mia helped Annie put her pink backpack on and grabbed Dylan's hand.

"Mom, this is a nice car," Corey said as he hopped in the front seat next to the driver. Mia sat in the back with Annie and Dylan. Corey turned to the driver. "*Salaam aleykum,*" he said.

"*Masha' Allah. Aleykum wassalaam.*" The driver grinned from ear to ear. "Are you Muslim?"

What kind of question was that? The driver knew that they were Christian. Mia waited to hear what Corey would say.

"*La, ana Masihiiya.* No, I'm a Christian."

Mia grinned. She didn't know if she was more proud of Corey's

Arabic skills or his stand for his beliefs. Well, yes, she did know.

The driver continued to chat with Corey as if he were an adult and not a nine year old. As much as the Arab culture irked her sometimes, there were also traits that impressed her. Older men mentoring the younger men was one of those traits. Even though it was to the exclusion of the women—just as the driver ignored Mia in the backseat—it was nice to see him treat Corey with dignity. Her son sat tall in the leather seat, as tall as he could with his legs not even touching the floor.

The plush sedan pulled up to the Westons' gate just after 3:30. What a day. Mia was tired and ready to get inside the house and relax. The first hour after school was the best time of the day because the three children had been away from each other all day so they got along well when they reunited. Mia thanked the driver and herded her kids out of the car and through the gate.

As she turned to nod a final thank you, she saw a man standing across the street talking on a cell phone. It wasn't unusual to see strangers on that street, but something about him caught her eye. Most people simply walked by because they were on their way somewhere. The man she saw was just standing there under a neem tree across from her house. Perhaps he was stopping for some shade. It was a hot day after all. Mia shrugged and closed the gate behind her.

Mia plopped on the couch with a large glass of water. She was so thirsty. She could hear the kids chattering in their bedroom. She smiled and leaned her head back. Perhaps she could take a small nap. It was already getting close to four in the afternoon, and if she was going to have dinner cooked and on the table by six, when Michael got home, she'd have to start now. Cooking from scratch took longer than opening cans and boxes like she would do if they lived in Texas. Mia sighed. So much for rest.

Before starting on dinner, Mia dialed Beth's number to check if she'd seen Michael. Beth didn't answer.

Definitely in a meeting then. I'll have dinner ready at six. Michael is bound to have had a challenging day. I'll not make an issue about the kids. Today is a day to extend grace.

Seven o'clock. The kids had eaten and Mia cleaned everything up except for the food and a place setting for Michael at the head of the table. Mia ignored the queasy feeling that surged in the pit of her stomach. She picked up the phone and dialed his number. His phone was off. It went straight to voicemail. She dialed Beth's and listened as it rang. On the fifth ring Beth answered.

"Hi, Beth, it's Mia. Hey, what time did Michael leave the office, do you know? He's not home yet but he never called to say he'd be late."

Beth paused a moment before responding. "Mia, he never came to the office today. I thought maybe he'd gone out to a refugee camp or something or maybe was working from home."

Mia's heart pounded in her chest. Beth's voice broke into Mia's spinning thoughts. "Mia, are you there? Listen, I'm coming over."

"Surely it's nothing. You are right, maybe he went to the camp."

"We are supposed to report at the office any time we go to the camp, and Michael never reported and never came in today. I'm coming over. I'll be there in half an hour."

Mia hung up the phone and sat stiffly on the couch. Michael was missing. What did it mean? *Hold yourself together, Mia. Just pray.*

"Mom?" Mia looked up and saw Corey standing in the doorway with a worried look on his face. "Is Dad working late tonight?"

Mia forced a smile. "Dad is tied up at the moment." Even as she said the words Mia hoped it wasn't literally true. "I'm not sure when he'll be home. It's better to just get ready for bed. He'll come tell you good night when he gets in."

"OK, I'll go take a bath." He turned to leave and Mia breathed a sigh of relief. No need to get the kids worried.

By the time Beth arrived, the kids were clean and headed to bed.

"Auntie Beth," they cried in unison when she walked in the door. Beth smiled and bent down to give Annie and Dylan bear hugs. She high-fived Corey.

"What are you doing here?" Corey asked. Was he getting suspicious that something was wrong? If he was, he didn't say anything.

"I'm here to keep your mom company until your dad gets home."

"Where's Daddy?" asked Annie.

"He's working of course," Dylan said, rolling his eyes as if he had to explain the obvious.

"Why don't you kids go get in your beds, and we'll pray?" Everyone filed into the bedroom that all three kids shared. The children slept in simple wooden framed beds arranged against three walls of the room. Mia's mother had made lightweight bedspreads for each of them. Dylan had a Disney-themed one, Annie had a princess-themed one, and Corey had a space-themed one. He used to have a superhero one, but he told Granny that now he was too old for cartoon characters. She made him a new one.

The kids obediently hopped in their beds while Beth and Mia stood in the doorway. "Corey, you pray for us," instructed Mia. Everyone but Mia bowed their heads and closed their eyes. Mia squeezed her eyes almost shut, but she peeked around the room as Corey prayed. She looked at her precious kids. She couldn't help but wonder. Was she a widow? Would she be raising these kids alone?

"Dear Jesus," Corey prayed, "Thank you for today. Thank you for Auntie Beth who's come to hang out with Mom. Please be with Dad . . . wherever he is tonight, and help him know You love him."

Mia gulped. Corey was always much wiser than Mia expected, and he often caught her off guard. He knew something was going on, but he had the wisdom to wait until she was ready to tell him. Now that was trust. *Do I trust God that much?*

Mia could hardly speak as she went from bed to bed to hug and kiss each child. She hugged a little tighter than usual this time, and she looked each child in the eye when she told them she loved them.

At the door, Mia turned, looked over the room, and smiled. What precious gifts these children were. She hoped their daddy was OK and that everything would go back to normal soon.

Beth and Mia sat in the living room. The children's room was just across the hall, so they spoke quietly.

"I made a few calls before I came," Beth said. "No one at the office knows where Michael was today. Habiib said they were supposed to meet for lunch, but Michael never showed up." She shook her head, "It's like the perfect storm. All these strange things happened, but no one thought anything about it, and now we look back and realize he's been missing all day. Did Michael actually say he was going to the office when he left this morning?"

Mia closed her eyes and tried to remember their conversation that morning. It had been just like any other morning. She couldn't remember anything different. She remembered their conversation over coffee. They talked about being seized by authorities as an opportunity to tell others about Jesus. But Mia didn't want to tell Beth about that. She wouldn't understand.

Still, Mia couldn't get the phrase out of her head. *But many who heard the message believed.* Was Michael in a situation where he was talking with police? Or a kidnapper? She had to pray for strength for him. She opened her eyes and saw Beth staring at her.

"No, he didn't say he was, but he didn't say he wasn't either, so I guess I just assumed . . ."

"Maybe he is in a meeting and forgot to tell you about it. Maybe his phone ran out of battery. Maybe we should go ahead and try to call him again."

Mia was certain he had planned to go to the office. He always told her if he had other plans. And she knew that he would have called her even if he had to use someone else's phone. Beth was trying to make her feel better and Mia appreciated it. The phrase that kept ringing in her head somehow comforted her more: *but many who heard the message believed.*

"Oh, Beth, I'm so sorry. I forgot to offer you a drink. You want some water?" Mia stood and walked to the kitchen without waiting for a reply. Sudanese hospitality had been drilled into her, and she always served water to guests. Beth followed her.

Mia filled a glass from the water filter and handed it to Beth. "I think I'll make some tea." She began to fill the teakettle with filtered water.

"Oh, no, I don't think I could drink any tea tonight. I feel like I drank about ten cups at my neighbor's house this afternoon."

"Well, I'm going to make it anyway." Mia continued filling the kettle. "I need a distraction." She set the kettle on the flame of the minisized cook stove and plopped two cinnamon sticks and three cardamom pods in the water to boil. *Halimah taught me to do that. She always made such good tea.*

Mia eyed the bowl of fermenting *aseeda* batter. The lumpy mixture was gray and thick bubbles formed around the edges like an evil monster was taking over.

"Mia?"

"Oh, sorry. Yes?"

"I was suggesting we try to call Michael again."

"All right. You try, my phone has a bad connection . . . keeps crackling when I make a phone call."

Beth punched numbers into her phone and held it to her ear.

"Nothing. Like it's turned off."

"Yeah, that's what it did to me too." Mia joined Beth sitting at the kitchen table. It was hot in the kitchen, even more so with the flame heating the water. The two friends sat in silence until steam rose from the kettle. Mia set two mugs on the counter. She filled a small sieve with loose tea leaves and held it over each mug as she poured the aromatic water over the tea, letting the water soak through the leaves and drip into each mug. Then she added two heaping spoons each of sugar and powdered milk into the mugs. Sweet Sudanese tea. Hard to beat.

They sat in the sweltering kitchen and sipped on the hot beverages. Somehow they didn't pay attention to the drops of sweat forming on their brows.

"I think we should report this," Beth said.

"To who? If the police took him, they already know."

"We don't know that it was police."

Beth was right. A couple of years earlier, an American man had been shot dead by renegade extremists. And even if it was the police, they didn't necessarily all work together or keep some sort of computerized spreadsheet of who they had arrested.

"I think it's best to call the police and report it. If it is them, at least they know we are worried and oppose this kind of treatment."

Mia nodded. "I think we need to call the Kellar Hope office in Dallas too." She remembered the embassy warning from that morning. "And the embassy as well."

This was good. At least they were doing something. Beth took the job of finding a number for the police and filing a report. Mia called the home office. Since Dallas was eight hours behind Khartoum time, people would be returning from lunch break. They decided to wait until the morning to call the embassy, as they could not find a 24-hour number.

The two eventually moved to the living room, and by midnight Beth had fallen asleep on the couch. Mia thought that was a miracle—the couch was locally purchased and definitely not made with comfort in mind. She planned to get some sleep herself, and tried to, but her mind would not stop racing. After half an hour of trying to sleep, she returned to the living room and, quietly as she could, turned on the computer.

Something had been nagging her all day. She kept pushing it to the back of her thoughts, but now that everyone was asleep and there was nothing to busy her, she decided to deal with it. Perhaps she already knew the answer.

When the computer screen lit up, Mia glanced behind her to see if the light bothered Beth. Her friend's eyes remained closed and she didn't stir. Mia turned back to the computer and brought up the Internet browser. Her fingers typed the words she'd been wondering all day.

How to know if your phone is tapped.

A list of possible sites popped up. Mia looked them over. She had no idea there would be so many sites with information like this. She clicked on one and skimmed the article until she found what she was looking for.

If you hear background noise, such as crackling, clicking, and the like, it is possible your phone has been bugged.

≥ Chapter 25 ≤

aylat alQadr. The Night of Power. Rania did not know when this special night would fall. No one did. The prophet Mohammed had never said for sure. The *sheikh* in Rania's neighborhood said it was one of the last ten nights of Ramadan, probably one of the odd-numbered nights. She could hear his old, cracking voice over the loud speaker now. He was reading verses from the Qur'an. Rania remembered the usual admonishments he broadcasted on Fridays: "You must stop your bad habits, and you must pray. You must rid your lives of evil: the evil of gossip, the evil of lying, the evil of associating with people from the West, especially *Amreeka*." His voice would reach a near glass-breaking shriek as he pronounced the final words. Then in a calmer voice he would say, "*Laylat alQadr* is a most blessed night. *Laylat alQadr* is more blessed than a thousand months. And you will be blessed if you are seeking Allah on that night. What you do on the Night of Power will be better than what you do in a thousand months. So be careful and mindful of the final nights of Ramadan."

Why would Allah be so cruel to promise a night of power but not tell us which night it is? Is He not our Creator? Doesn't He know that humans cannot stay up all night for ten nights in a row? Rania did not voice the questions to anyone; instead, they danced in her head like flies on a mound of meat at the local butcher where Mama shopped. Just like the butcher did to the flies, Rania brushed the thoughts away, knowing they would return.

She distracted her mind by looking at her drawings. What should she draw next? She remembered the conversation she'd had with Jamal in her own doorway. That was the night she'd first imagined being married to him. That was the night she thought perhaps everything would work out OK after all. She and Jamal could seek *Isa* together.

But that was not to be. Rania sighed. She took out her pencils and propped her drawing book against her knees as she sat on her bed and leaned against the wall. She sketched the shape of a door. It looked like the metal gate where she and Jamal talked. She drew the door shut.

Maybe she would even add the padlock that her father used to lock it at night. The door to freedom with Jamal was certainly shut and locked. Her picture might as well show it that way too.

Rania leaned her head back and closed her eyes. Why did her thoughts go back to Jamal the way they did? She thought about Jamal's dreams. She wondered if he would have more. Sometimes people had dreams during *Laylat alQadr*. Would Jamal have another dream? Would she have a dream?

It was said that if a Muslim were praying and seeking Allah on *Laylat alQadr* all their past sins would be forgiven. That was the holiest night, after all: the night that the Qur'an was first revealed to the prophet Mohammed.

Which night is it? I would like to know the truth about Isa *and all that I am reading in the book about Him. I wonder if Allah will tell me if I ask Him on* Laylat alQadr?

A knock on the door interrupted Rania's thoughts. The door opened, and her father walked in and stood awkwardly in the doorway. He didn't often come into Rania's room—not since the night Halimah was caught with all the Christian books.

"Rania, we will break the fast with Uncle Asim and Auntie Fareeda tonight."

"Father, I don't want to go."

"*Habeebtee*, my dear." Father's words were kind. "You need to get out of the house. You have hardly done anything since Mama went to visit Haboba."

"I don't want to go see them. Bashir will not be there, and seeing them without Bashir will just make me sad."

"*Habeebtee*, you know that they left Bashir with a *sheikh* when they moved back to Khartoum. He is in good hands. The *sheikh* will take care of him."

Rania did not agree. The *sheikh* in the village would not take care of Bashir. Her cousin was mentally ill and needed help. Everyone in the family, except Rania and Halimah, said that Bashir was demon-possessed and needed a *sheikh* to read the Qur'an to him. Arguing with Father would only make him mad, so Rania kept her thoughts to herself.

"I want to stay home, Father. Please?"

Father sighed. "OK."

Rania jumped up from the bed, sending her pencils scattering on the floor. She tiptoed and kissed him on the cheek.

"Thank you, Father."

He smiled and patted her cheek. "My precious daughter."

Rania's chest tightened. She kept a smile on her face, but her heart ached. *You have another daughter, too, Father. Don't forget Halimah.*

⁕⁕⁕

Father, Abdu, and Ali left the house in midafternoon to drive across town. Father wanted to arrive at Uncle Asim's house before the call to prayer that broke the fast. Everyone else in Khartoum, of course, did the same thing, so traffic was congested as buses, cars, rickshaws, and taxis jockeyed for positions on the dusty crumbling streets around town.

In the quiet of the empty home, Rania called Mama on the house phone.

"Rania? *Habeebtee*? Is everything OK?"

"Yes, Mama. I just wanted to hear your voice. How is Haboba?"

"She is still very sick. I don't know if there is much we can do for her. She is very old, you know. Maybe Allah is willing that her life here is done."

"Mama, don't say that."

"If Allah wills it, who are we to argue?"

"When will you come home?" Rania changed the subject. She hadn't expected Mama to say Haboba was dying. Rania didn't think she could handle another loss. She wanted Mama to come home and for everything to go back to normal.

"I don't know yet, *habeebtee*. I need to stay with Haboba a while longer."

"So, will you be home for *Eid al-Fitr*, the festival at the end of Ramadan? It's only ten days away."

"I don't know yet."

Rania sighed. "OK. Please tell Haboba I love her. Mama?"

"Yes?"

"You know how Haboba says that *Laylat alQadr* is the twenty-seventh night of Ramadan? Do you think that is true?"

"*Insha' Allah, habeebtee.* If God wills."

Rania hung up the phone. Tonight was the twentieth night of Ramadan. Since that was within the last ten days of the lunar month, it was possible that tonight was the true *Laylat alQadr.* Should she stay up all night and seek Allah?

When the call to prayer rang out over the neighborhood, Rania went to the kitchen and drank some water and ate leftovers from the night before. All across Khartoum families were gathering to eat and break the fast together. Across town her own father and brothers were feasting over food and fellowship.

An hour later there was a knock at the gate. Rania threw a scarf over her head as she walked across the outer courtyard. Probably some neighbor asking to borrow sugar or perhaps a handful of tea leaves.

She gulped when she saw the form of Jamal standing there as she opened the gate. She hadn't seen his handsome figure since she'd heard the news of his engagement.

"*Salaam aleykum,*" he said in his deep voice. The voice of one who would never be her husband.

"*Aleykum wassalaam.*" She muttered. "What are you doing here? Father is not around."

"Actually, I know that already. I came because I wanted to tell you something."

"You can't come in."

"Of course not, Rania. I know that." He seemed offended that she would suggest it. Rania was sorry she'd sounded so presumptuous. "I wanted to tell you that I believe in *Isa.* I think He is the way to God. I think you should believe the things you are reading in the book. I was able to get a copy of all the books the Christians read. It is called *Kitab alMuqaddas,* the Holy Book. I believe it is all true."

"Wow, that's a big secret to tell me, Jamal. Why don't you just tell it to your fiancée?" Rania heard the bite in her tone.

"Because she does not believe in *Isa*. She is a good Muslim and will never change."

"Then why marry her?" Rania hoped she wasn't whining. That would give away her disappointment and she would not let Jamal know she was disappointed.

"Because it is what my family wants, Rania. I just want you to know that I do believe that *Isa* is the way to God."

Rania wrinkled her nose. "Have you told your family?"

"No, of course not. I am going to remain Muslim but also believe in *Isa*."

"I don't know what you've read, Jamal, but from what I've read I don't think you can do that. *Isa* says 'I am the way' and 'No one comes to the Father except through me.'"

"Why can't I? Muslims and Christians are almost the same. When I pray in the mosque, my heart will be praying to *Isa*."

He spoke with such confidence. Maybe he was right. Maybe she could be both. Then she wouldn't be beaten and cast out from the family like Halimah had been.

"I don't know, Jamal. Seems dishonest."

Jamal's voice was agitated. "I'm not asking your permission, Rania. I am just telling you. You are the only person who knows about this. And I'm guessing I'm the only one who knows you are reading that book. And I think we are way past being honest with our families."

"Have you had any more dreams, Jamal?"

"Not lately." He sounded disappointed.

"*Laylat alQadr* is coming. It could even be tonight. Maybe you will have a dream then." Rania's voice was thoughtful. "As Muslims, on the night of *Laylat alQadr*, if we are praying, we can have all our past sins forgiven. But *Isa* says that He can forgive sins. Who is telling the truth?"

"Since you already know my secret, I will tell you the truth. I think *Isa* is the One who can forgive our sins."

"If you believe that, why won't you tell your family?"

"Because I don't want to lose my family. I need to go, they are waiting on me. *Masa 'ilxayr.* Good night."

He turned and walked away, not even waiting for a reply. Rania didn't bother to give one. She shut the gate. She didn't want to watch her almost-husband fade away from her sight. She walked back into the house and sat on a chair in the salon—her father's chair, where he always sat when Jamal came to visit.

Is Jamal right? Can I be Muslim and Christian at the same time? Can I believe in Isa *and keep it a secret? Who can I ask that can help me sort out all this confusion?*

Rania pulled the scarf from her hair, put her head in her hands, and cried. The boom of music from next door filled her ears. *Must be Ali's friends in their courtyard listening to that crazy hip-hop music.* It reminded her of Maysoon. If Rania were honest, she'd tell Maysoon that the music drove her crazy. Who liked hip-hop anyway? She thought about that night she watched Maysoon sing with her group. She'd sat there awkward and alone, trying to support her friend. Well, mostly alone, except for when that white lady and her son had come over. Rania jumped up from the chair, dropping her scarf to the floor.

For once, she was alone in the house. This was the perfect time to call the number on the piece of paper. She ran to her bedroom and dug through her bag. Was it still there? Had it fallen out? Oh, please let it not have fallen out.

Her fingers felt a piece of paper buried at the bottom of her bag. She grabbed it and pulled it out. She'd stuffed it in her bag and then, in the craziness that had been her life lately, she'd forgotten all about it.

Unfolding it she read the word, "Halimah" followed by a string of numbers—too many numbers for a local number. What country was this phone number from? Should Rania try it? Surely a foreign number would be expensive to call. Her heart sank.

Maybe she could try to text it. She grabbed her cell phone and entered the number. What would she say? What if it was a trick?

Rania pushed away her fears and she typed the words "This is Rania" into her phone and hit the *send* button.

Rania prayed five times a day for all the final days of Ramadan. Jamal would have been proud. Maysoon would have scoffed at her. Halimah? She didn't know what Halimah would think. The older sister never replied to Rania's text.

It was the twenty-seventh day of Ramadan. She had tried to stay up all night on the twentieth and even a couple of other nights after that but had always fallen asleep. But she pushed her guilty feelings aside because surely tonight was *Laylat alQadr*, the Night of Power. Every day Rania had prayed the obligatory prayers, prayers she had recited from memory from the time she was just a little girl. But when she finished, she would add her own prayer. *Allah, please show me the truth on Laylat alQadr.* Tonight was the night, just as Haboba said. *Insha' Allah*, her prayers would be answered.

Father, Abdu, and Ali would observe *itikaf* at the mosque tonight. They would be praying and listening to the reading of the Qur'an all night long, in hopes of getting a special message on this most holy night. Would she get a message tonight? She genuinely hoped so. A lot was banking on her getting a message from Allah tonight. She was tired of watching everyone else and wondering who was right.

Was Halimah right? She'd been beaten up and cast out of the family, but she earnestly told Rania the book was true. Or was Maysoon right? She was free from the rules of Islam, but she was no longer under the safety and shelter of her family. She was chasing a hip-hop dream. What about Haboba? She'd diligently followed Islam all her life and never once questioned it. Now she was nearing death. Did she wonder in her heart if Allah would be merciful and let her into paradise? Did Amal have the best answer of all? Just kill herself and be done with all the questions. Rania wanted to believe Halimah. She wanted to believe the book was true. Perhaps Allah would tell her tonight if she prayed all night.

The sun glared angrily down at Rania as she walked toward the main road to catch a bus. Unfortunately, she'd had to lie to Father.

"I'm going to the *souq*, the market, to pick up some things we need for *Eid al-Fitr*."

"You know it is inappropriate to go alone. Take Ali with you."

"I want to go quickly, Father. Ali will only get in the way. Please let me go alone. I won't be gone long."

To her surprise, Father had agreed. She needed to make this a quick trip and be home even sooner than Father expected so he wouldn't get suspicious. She hailed the city bus and waited for the decrepit vehicle to pull to a stop on the side of the dusty road. A young boy hung out the door, one hand clutched the rusting frame and one hand held old dirty bills that stuck out from between each finger like a fan of money. She handed him her bus fare and sat in the nearest empty seat.

Ten minutes later, Rania snapped her fingers in the customary way, and the bus creaked to the side of the road again. She hopped down and shielded her face with the edge of her scarf as dust kicked up by the departing bus blew about her. As it settled she saw the smiling face of Maysoon.

"You made it," her friend said.

"I made it." She smiled and then looked around her. "So, you live here?" Her friend pointed to the large nondescript two-story building. The bottom floor housed an assortment of stores: a small appliance shop, a teashop, a radio repair shop, and a butcher. Rania looked at the second and third floor. People in the city sometimes lived in buildings like this. It's not that it was bad to live above a row of shops. But for a single girl?

Maysoon smiled and grabbed Rania's hand. "Come on, I'll show you." She led the way up a dark dirty set of stairs to the third floor. As she walked, she chattered. "I live next door to two German girls who work for their embassy."

Rania could see by the way Maysoon dressed that she had been influenced by her neighbors. She still covered her hair with a *tarha*. But her jeans were a little too tight, and her blouse showed a little too much of her arm. Maysoon's father would not have approved.

The beat of pop music thumped from the neighbors' apartment as

Maysoon twisted a large skeleton key in her own door. She leaned her shoulder in and gave the door a firm shove before it reluctantly creaked open and let them in. The girls stepped inside, and Maysoon stood in the room with a grin, proudly showing off her new home.

It was dark and smelled musty. Rania could see that there was a small kitchenette in the back and a second door, perhaps to a bathroom. In the room where they stood, she saw a metal bed on the left. A mosquito net hung over the simple frame, held up by a hook on the wall. On the right two plastic chairs and a small metal table with paint chipping off the legs pretended to be a sitting area.

Rania wanted to be supportive of her friend, but this was such a far cry from her parents' nice home across town. "Do your parents know this is where you are living?"

"Not exactly. I told them I was going to move in with Mel for a few weeks because it's quiet at her house so I'll be able to study better."

"Mel? From the Jadeed Cultural Center?"

"Well, I told them she is a new religion teacher at school." Maysoon gave a sheepish grin.

"*Ya salaam.* They will never believe that."

"My mother is so busy with all the little ones, I think she was relieved I found a place to focus on finishing school."

Rania shook her head in disbelief. This was never going to work. "Can we turn on a light so I can see better?" she asked, wiping sweat from her face with the edge of her *tarha*. Why didn't Maysoon turn on the air-conditioner?

"The power is out right now. It's OK, I can open the window." Maysoon wrestled with a green metal shutter on the wall by the chairs and table until she got it to open. The sound of cars and buses on the street wafted in, along with dust and more heat.

"If there's no power, how can your neighbors play their music?"

"Oh, they have a generator. That's why they turn the volume of the music up, to cover the noise of that loud machine. They can't go very long without an air-conditioner." Maysoon laughed. "They are soft."

I must be soft too, then. It's like an oven in here.

"What's this stuff?" Rania pointed to a metal box with flowers painted all over it. Next to it was a cardboard box that appeared to be bulging.

"Oh, that. Just wait . . ." She took the short metal stool that sat upside down on top of the cardboard box and placed it on the floor. Sitting on it she dragged the metal box in front of her and then looked up at Rania and smiled. "Meet Maysoon the Tea Lady."

"What are you talking about?"

"I'm going to be a tea lady. That's how I'm going to make money to earn enough to leave Sudan."

"Maysoon, you can't be a tea lady."

"Why not?" Maysoon asked, eyebrows raised.

"It's just not . . . well it's not—" Rania searched for words.

"Not what we Arab girls do? Not what a good Muslim girl does? Is it beneath me, Rania?" Maysoon was now standing with her hands on her hips.

"It's not safe for you, Maysoon. That's what."

"So it's safer to just stay in my parents' home and do whatever they say and never have a life of my own? If that is what safety is, I don't want to be safe."

"Maysoon, don't be ridiculous. A tea lady is not a good job. You know tea ladies have a bad reputation. You know how our fathers and brothers speak about tea ladies. Do you want men to talk about you that way?"

"Who cares what they say? If it's not true, it doesn't matter. I'm not going to do anything bad. I'm just going to sit on the street and make tea for people."

"For men. Women don't go to tea ladies."

"Well, for whoever wants to buy tea. Good grief, Rania, you sure know how to ruin things."

Guilt made Rania's chest ache. She hadn't meant to discourage her friend. She reached out and grabbed Maysoon's hand.

"Just be careful," she said. "I worry about you, that's all."

"Don't worry about me, Rania. 'I've made up my mind. I've listened to enough advice, I know what I need to find.'" She quoted the lyrics from

Freedom's hip-hop song, and as she did so, Rania knew there was no changing her friend's mind.

An hour later, Rania hopped on a bus and rode home. As her body bounced on the dirty vinyl bus seat, she looked out the window and waved to her friend. Was running away really freedom? *What do I want? Is it freedom? Is it marriage to Jamal? Is it the approval of my family?*

Without thinking, she reached up to the glass pane of the bus window and traced her finger in the dust. Her finger swirled from right to left as she wrote the Arabic word *salaam*. Peace. That's what she wanted. Her neighborhood was a hotbed of gossip with all that had happened over the past year. Was there any neighborhood in any other part of town that had endured as much scathing drama as hers?

Everyone seemed to be looking for something, and no one seemed satisfied. Lies, gossip, dishonesty—so much sin hidden just under the surface. Every person, including Rania, was just like Amal's house: clean walls on the outside, but a dirty and sad house on the inside. Could Allah really be pleased with such a confused neighborhood of people? Not one of them had done enough good deeds to warrant Allah's mercy on the Day of Judgment. Even if every single one of them stayed up all night tonight, the Night of Power, would Allah even care to overlook their bad deeds and reward them for their good ones?

Peace. She'd read about peace in the book. "Peace I leave with you; my peace I give you. I do not give to you as the world gives. Do not let your hearts be troubled and do not be afraid." That's what Rania wanted. She didn't understand what *Isa* meant by those words. It sounded too good to be true. But she had an idea, and it grew within her like a burgeoning vine that swirled through her heart and mind and emotions, gripping her thoughts until she knew she'd have to try it.

I will stay up all night tonight. I will find out once and for all. Tonight, after the evening prayers, I will ask Allah to show me a sign. I will ask Allah to tell me what is true. Is Mohammed true? Is Isa true? If I can find peace, then that is all I want.

Rania smiled as she gazed through the smudged window. The mud-brick houses and the white-robed men she passed along the side of the road were blurry through the dirty glass. But in her mind, Rania's thoughts were as clear as the sky on a cloudless day. Tonight she would find an answer once and for all.

≫ Chapter 27 ≪

M ommy?"
      Mia rolled over and saw Annie standing beside her bed.

"Mommy? Are you awake?" The little girl crawled into the bed beside Mia. Her hair was a tangled mass of blond curls. Her eyes were sleepy and her body still warm from her own bed. She snuggled up next to Mia. Mia loved snuggles, but Sudan was much too hot for that.

"Aren't you hot, Annie?"

Annie sat up and looked across the bed. "Where's Daddy?"

It all came flooding back to Mia. The day of phone calls with no answers. The evening of waiting for Michael. The search on the Internet. The hours of fitful sleep. Her head ached. She lifted her hand to her temple, feeling her own mass of tangled blond curls.

"Where's Daddy, Mommy?" Annie persisted.

Mia hadn't planned what she would tell the children yet. She dragged herself out of the bed.

"Annie, why don't you go get dressed, and when we sit down for breakfast I'll tell you where Daddy is?"

That seemed to satisfy the little girl, and she skipped to her bedroom.

Wait, what time is it?

Mia had been flustered by the sudden waking and then by the realization that what had happened yesterday was not a nightmare but reality. She hadn't even looked at the clock. Mia glanced at her bedside table. Six o'clock in the morning. This was confirmed by the sudden beeping of her alarm clock. It was time to meet with Michael for coffee and Bible reading. She looked at the bed. Michael's side was empty. Somehow she'd hoped he would be there.

It was too early for the kids to wake up, but now that Annie had bounced off to the room, the other two would be awake in no time. Once they saw Beth on the couch, they'd want an explanation. Perhaps it was good that they were up early enough to spend a little extra time explaining things. But what was she going to say?

Mia piled dirty breakfast bowls in the sink. Tzega would arrive soon, so she didn't have to wash them. Dylan would be a helpful distraction for her. At four years old, he did not comprehend that anything serious was going on. Mia's explanation at breakfast that "Daddy was busy with some things, probably talking to some people about his job" was good enough for him. He jabbered his way through breakfast and followed Beth closely as she washed her face and tidied the living room.

Corey and Annie, however, had picked up on a problem. Annie was quiet at breakfast and afterward, as the children organized their backpacks for school, Mia heard Corey comforting her. "Don't worry, Annie. God is with Dad. And God is with us too. If you get worried while we are at school, just pray. That's what Mom always does."

Mia's heart melted. Corey was so mature. Was he really only nine years old?

Beth took the older children to school and said she'd go home and change clothes then go to the office to see if she could find out any information. Beth was a lifesaver—or at least a sanity-saver during the long hours since they realized Michael was missing.

Dylan looked at picture books on the master bed while Mia took a shower. He wouldn't stay in one spot for long. Mia locked the bathroom door and stepped under the water to enjoy a few moments of solitude. The lukewarm water seeped through her hair and ran down her body like a refreshing rain. She needed to think clearly. She needed answers.

Where is he, Lord? Where is he?

She wanted to pray for wisdom and courage for Michael, but her thoughts could not express it. All she could manage to pray was, *Where is he, Lord? Lord, help us.* She hoped God would understand the prayers she couldn't say.

Mia toweled off and dressed. She wanted to be ready to dash out the door if there was news about Michael, so she chose a long black skirt and a cotton shirt with midlength sleeves. When she opened the door, Dylan was sitting quietly on the bed, just where she'd left him.

Thank You, Lord. She did not have time for an unruly four year old.

She desperately hoped he would be cooperative and obedient today.

"I think I hear Miss Tzega coming in the gate, Dylan. Why don't you run out and greet her?"

Dylan set the book down and jumped off the bed. He ran toward the front door yelling, "*Sabah 'ilxayr.* Good morning."

Tzega entered the house holding Dylan's hand. She smiled at Mia. "*Sabah 'ilxayr.*"

"*Sabah 'innoor,*" Mia responded. *Morning of light.* But it didn't really feel like a morning of light. Maybe she should have said "morning of panic." But that wasn't a very polite greeting was it? Mia didn't mention Michael. Better not say anything until they knew what was going on.

Dylan joined Tzega in the kitchen as she washed the breakfast dishes. Usually Mia would spend this time checking email or straightening her room. She didn't want to check email. Wherever Michael was, he didn't have access to email, so why check? She didn't want to see an embassy warden's message or a letter from her mom. She didn't want to decide if she was going to tell her family what was going on. She didn't want to straighten her room either because she didn't want to see the bed she'd slept alone in the night before, although *sleep* was a generous term.

Mia walked outside and looked around the front yard. The rose bushes were blooming, and the lime tree was beginning to produce little white buds that would soon turn into limes. Mia didn't notice any of that. She walked to the front gate and opened it just a tiny bit. Peering out the crack, she saw the same mystery man she'd seen before. Today he had a plastic chair and was sitting on the broken sidewalk across the street reading a newspaper. Mia closed the gate and leaned against it.

Is he spying on us? The house phone is tapped. Michael is missing. Oh, Lord, please help me. Mia forced herself to walk back inside the house and down the hall to her bedroom. She was going to do the things she normally did until she knew what else to do. She was determined to make her bed. Mia took Dylan's books off the bed and stacked them neatly on her bedside table. She ignored the fact that one side of the bed had not been slept in and smoothed out the sheets as if it had. She pulled the covers up and fluffed the pillows.

As she worked, Mia could hear Tzega singing in the kitchen. Dylan was trying to sing along with her. But she sang in her native tongue, so he just made up words. In spite of the worry that filled her heart, Mia smiled. She remembered her conversation with Tzega just the day before: *We pray that he is in Massawa. At the prison in Massawa, they do not beat the prisoners as badly as at the other prisons.* And yet, there she was singing with Dylan, as if life was simple and happy.

Mia took her Bible from the bedside table and sat on the veranda. It was hot outside, but it was hot inside too. Either way she was going to sweat, so she decided to sweat outside where at least she could hear the birds chirping in the lime tree.

She opened her Bible to Acts and reread the first four chapters. It was hard to concentrate. She wanted Beth to call so they could make a plan, and she could do something besides sit and wait.

Beth did call with some news. Mia's phone crackled as she listened to her friend's voice.

"I reported to the office that Michael was missing, and Habiib called to check with the police. The police are asking for Michael's passport. It wasn't exactly clear, Mia, but I think the police may have Michael."

"What do you mean the police have him? How can they arrest him? He hasn't done anything." Mia's voice verged on panic.

Beth spoke calmly. "Mia, remember, we don't have any rights here. It's a different game. We have to play by their rules."

"What are their rules?"

Beth sighed. "Anything they want them to be. Look, I think you need to give them his passport. You need to be compliant. I'll come by in a few minutes and get it."

"OK." Mia's voice deflated. Was there no recourse? Was she just supposed to do whatever they wanted? She hadn't called the embassy yet. Mia sat up straight in the plastic chair, knocking her Bible from her lap. The embassy. This gave Mia some energy.

She quickly retrieved Michael's passport from their bedroom. They kept their passports in a small handbag that they called their "go bag." This was a bag with all passports, cash, important documents, and a change of clothes for each member of the family. If Khartoum ever got into a situation that required quick evacuation of Americans, the Westons were ready. The "go bag" was not something Mia ever told her family back home about, but it was standard practice for Americans living in Khartoum.

With Michael's passport in hand, Mia found the number for the US consulate on the Internet. She added the number to the contacts in her phone. It was a good idea to have it easily accessible. She'd wait for Beth to arrive before calling.

Her flurry of action brought calm to Mia. She began to pray for Michael and for the police who had him. She prayed for Beth, for Corey and Annie, for Dylan, for Tzega. She was surprised how quickly the time passed until Beth arrived.

"I have the number for the consulate," Mia said. "Should I call them now?"

"Well," Beth said. "Now that we think he is with the police, let's wait and see what is going on."

"Really?" Mia was incredulous. "This is serious. They took him for no reason. The embassy needs to know that."

Beth remained calm, and rather than frustrating her, it soothed Mia. "Yes, the embassy needs to know. But we don't know exactly what they need to know yet. Let's find out what's going on, then we can report it."

"OK, that makes sense . . . I think. It's not like I've done this before," Mia smiled weakly. She handed Michael's passport to her friend. "This feels pretty dangerous giving up his passport. I hope they give it back."

"Me too," Beth said. "Do you have a photocopy of it?"

Mia nodded.

Beth hugged Mia. "It's going to be all right. God's in control of even this, you know?"

"I know He is. Thanks." Mia walked Beth to the front gate and waved as she drove away. The mystery man sat reading the newspaper. He ignored her.

Mia distracted herself by working on her *aseeda* project. She boiled a pan of water and poured in the sour-smelling substance. After five minutes of stirring, she guessed that the porridge was thick enough, so she transferred it into the plastic mold. She washed the dirty dishes and then eyed the *aseeda*. Surely it was cool enough to turn onto the platter like Hanaan had taught her. She grabbed the bowl and carefully turned it upside down. The substance slurped as she lifted the bowl. Instead of a neat round shape of dough, gray globs spread out onto the platter.

Tears filled Mia's eyes. She sat at the kitchen table with her head in her hands and cried.

⁓⁓⁓

Beth offered to pick Corey and Annie up from school so when the time got close for them to arrive home, Mia had rehearsed her explanation.

"Daddy is still not home, but we know who he is talking to, and they will let him come back soon. But you know what? Let's pray for him right now."

That satisfied the children and after a prayer—that Mia somehow managed to voice without crying—they ran off to play in their bedroom.

Not only had Beth fetched the children from school, she'd stopped by a restaurant to pick up *shawarmas*, Middle-Eastern-style chicken wraps, for Mia and the kids. This was good since Mia's *aseeda* had failed. Mia was grateful her friend had stuck to helping her with logistics and refrained from any sort of I-told-you-not-to-be-so-bold speech.

➣ Chapter 28 ➢

A nd then it was over, just like that. As the sun began to lower in the sky, Mia heard the creak of the gate. She was in the kitchen, and by the time she'd taken off her apron and walked to the front door, Michael had already opened the gate for himself and pulled the car into the driveway.

"Daddy's home," Mia yelled as she waited for all three kids to come barreling to the door.

The children squealed and ran into the yard, each trying to be the first one to get a hug. Michael smiled and hugged each one of them, longer than usual, Mia noted. Then he walked up to Mia and gave her the longest hug of all. He smelled sweaty and dirty. Mia looked into his tired eyes, not daring to ask any questions in front of the children.

"Corey," Michael said, "your mom and I have some catching up to do, why don't you take the other two and go play?"

"OK, Dad." Corey turned to his siblings. "Come on, let's finish building the block city." His enthusiasm was contagious, and the other two followed happily. To them, Dad was home again, and all was good with the world.

"You're safe," Mia said, hugging Michael again. "I was so worried."

"I was afraid you would be," Michael said, holding her. "To be honest, I was a little concerned myself."

"They just let you go?"

"Yes, with no explanation. It was as if that had been the arrangement all along."

"Why did they keep you in the first place?"

"They never said. But they asked me questions about Kellar Hope, such as the names of employees and information about the refugee camps we worked in. It was all stuff they could have found out by simply walking into the office and asking any secretary."

"They can't just keep you for no reason."

"Yes, they can. They can do whatever they want. They can make up the rules as they go if they want to. We don't have a say in it."

"So what now? Do they want us to leave?"

"They didn't say that. They even gave me my passport back." He held up the little blue booklet and managed a smile.

Mia sighed. The passport was a valuable commodity. Without it, they couldn't travel anywhere.

"Well, why don't you take a shower, and I'll make you some food."

"That would be great. I'd like to get out of these clothes. And eat something besides hot tea and bread."

"Is that all they gave you?"

"Yep."

Anger, with a smidgen of fear, welled up inside Mia. Did they just wake up in the morning and, while drinking their morning cup of tea, decide which *khawadja* they were going to intimidate that day?

⁕⁕⁕⁕⁕

Sloppy joes were on the menu for dinner. Since it was not quite dinner-time yet, Mia didn't call the children. She let them play while she served Michael two sandwiches and a bowl of homemade potato chips at the kitchen table.

She watched him as he ate. He looked and smelled better after having showered and dressed in clean clothes. Was he thinner than before?

"I should tell you that I think the phone is tapped."

Mia described what she'd found on the Internet. They agreed to be extra discreet when using it.

Michael described more about his experience. The police had not been outright mean to him. But now that he was back home, he described subtle forms of intimidation: sitting and waiting for long hours in a dark room without ventilation, only tea and bread to eat. Simple things—almost undetectable—but on further inspection, definitely passive aggressive.

"It's as if they walk right up to the line of what's acceptable and linger there. That makes their tactics easy to deny and difficult to prove."

Corey poked his head into the kitchen and eyed Michael's plate. "Did y'all eat without us?"

Mia forced a smile. "I was just letting Dad eat first. Why don't you help me set the dining room table, and we can eat there?"

Michael sat with the family for dinner, and Mia saw that he tried to interact with the kids, asking questions and listening to stories. But he was distracted. His eyes betrayed fatigue and discouragement.

Mia instructed the kids to help her clear the table. Then she directed them through baths and getting ready for bed. "Annie, go in our bedroom, and tell Daddy that it's time for bedtime prayers."

A few moments later Annie returned to the kids' bedroom where Mia and the boys were setting out clothes for the next day. "Daddy's already asleep."

"OK, we'll just pray without him."

"Is Dad OK, Mom?" Corey asked. He was definitely getting old enough to sense when things were amiss.

"He's just tired."

"Then let's pray for him," Dylan said, as he crawled into his bed, pulling the covers up to his chin.

"Let's do that." Mia faked a smile. She couldn't pray out loud right now. The kids would definitely sense that something was wrong. "Annie, you pray for us."

"Dear God, thank you that Daddy is home. Thank you for taking care of him when we couldn't. Help us to sleep real good tonight so that Mommy and Daddy can feel happy again tomorrow. In Jesus' name, amen."

Mia choked back tears. She wanted faith like Annie's. She wanted to believe that God was taking care of them, even when they couldn't take care of themselves because the rules had somehow changed, and they were at the mercy of those in charge of this country.

Mia hugged each child, kissing them on the cheek and telling them how much she and their dad loved them. Then she flipped off the light switch and went to her bedroom. Michael, fully dressed, was sprawled out on the bed. She changed into a nightgown, turned off the light, and crawled into bed. It was still early, but she was exhausted too. At least tonight she wouldn't have to sleep alone, not knowing where her husband was. She hoped she never had to do that again.

<center>~~~~~</center>

"Let the morning bring me word of your unfailing love, for I have put my trust in you."

"Excuse me?" Mia blinked and looked up. Reality came flooding back to her. The voice was Michael's, and as she turned her head toward the sound, she saw him standing by her side of the bed, holding a cup of coffee for her.

She grunted sleepily as she hoisted herself up and leaned against the headboard. Michael grinned and handed the steaming cup to her.

"What time is it?"

"Six o'clock."

"How long have you been awake?"

"About an hour."

"Michael, why didn't you sleep in? You must be exhausted."

"In body, yes. But I needed time in the Word more than I needed sleep. I was reading Psalm 143. 'Let the morning bring me word of your unfailing love, for I have put my trust in you. Show me the way I should go, for to you I entrust my life.' Mia, I think the Lord has shown me the way we should go."

Mia was still sleepy, still trying to jump start her brain, like their old creaky generator outside that had to be coaxed into motion when there was a power outage.

"We should go? You mean leave Sudan?"

Yes, he's right. We probably should. There are just too many things working against us right now. The guys at the office, Beth, Kellar Hope, and now the police.

"No, actually. The exact opposite." Michael's words flowed with speed and enthusiasm. He was buzzing on something more than coffee. "I was also reading in 1 Corinthians. Paul writes that 'a great door for effective work has opened to me, and there are many who oppose me.'"

Mia took a gulp of coffee, hoping its effect would be immediate. "So what are you saying?"

Michael hopped onto the opposite side of the bed and sat next to her. "I'm saying that opposition does not mean closed doors. I'm saying God has given us so many amazing opportunities to share the news of Jesus and His forgiveness with people who never knew that salvation was an option for them. I'm saying we have a great door for effective work."

"And there are many who oppose us."

"Yes. But that doesn't mean we quit. God brought us here. Remember, back in Texas, when we really wanted to move overseas, but we thought a possibility would never come up? Remember when we got a letter from Dr. Kellar, telling us about the opportunity in Khartoum? We felt like it was a miracle. We felt like God had orchestrated that for us."

"Yes, I remember."

"If God did that to get us here, don't you think He can keep us here if He wants to?"

"What about the police?"

"What about them? Haven't we always known that being hassled by the police was a possibility? Look what God did; He rescued us. We aren't being forced to leave. They didn't do anything."

Mia felt confidence building in her spirit. Was it the coffee? Was it the Scripture? She sat up and took her Bible from the bedside table.

"I was reading in Acts 19." Mia looked sheepishly at Michael. "I read ahead while you were . . . gone. The story is about Paul in Ephesus, and he really ruffled some feathers there. I realized that the spreading of the gospel is messy. Not neat and clean like I imagine it to be."

Michael nodded. "It's messy and sometimes scary. Like Halimah's situation . . . and like what happened to us. But God is always sovereign."

"I used to think that *effective* meant things go smoothly, with no bumps in the road. But it's obvious here in Sudan that bumps in the road and effectiveness go together."

Michael grabbed her hand. "Babe, I think we should stay."

More than ever before, Mia felt settled in her spirit. Settled because she knew that they were giving up all their rights. Not to Sudan. Not to the police. They had surrendered their rights, giving them to God Himself. He was sovereign. He made a way for them to come to Sudan.

He would make a way for them to stay. And when it was time to go back to Texas, He would make that clear as well. To rely on anything less than that would be to give in to the "many that oppose."

Somehow, in surrendering everything, Mia felt freer than she had in a long time.

⇒ Chapter 29 ⇐

Work at Kellar Hope slowed to a turtle's pace during the month of Ramadan. Schools revised their schedules to accommodate the Muslim students who stayed up most of the night, so the children only attended classes from ten in the morning until two in the afternoon.

By decree of the government, along with societal pressure, no one could eat or drink in public. Restaurants closed down until late at night, and some closed completely for the entire month of fasting.

A sleepy city went to work for a couple of hours every morning, but by midmorning people were too tired to labor. Storekeepers laid their heads on the countertops, street workers sprawled on the edge of the road, and even the grocery store workers who stocked shelves leaned lazily against the boxes of groceries they were hired to unpack.

The late afternoons during Ramadan were dangerous. Those who owned cars sped carelessly toward home in order to make it in time for *iftaar*, the breaking of the fast at sunset. Every year multiple vehicle accidents occurred because of hungry drivers with only the one goal in mind.

Most of the month of Ramadan, if they hadn't been invited to *iftaar* with anyone, Mia and her family stayed home from the late afternoon on. It wasn't that she went anywhere when it wasn't Ramadan, but the fact that she couldn't go anywhere for a full month frustrated her.

That's why, toward the end of the month, she was so thankful for the evening that Hanaan invited the family for *iftaar*. It wasn't a trip across town, but at least visiting her neighbors got her out of her own house.

Her excitement was dampened slightly by Michael's mood. He came home from the office grumpy and grew quiet and distant. They were supposed to be social tonight. This was one of the few times Michael had ever been around Hanaan's husband. Mia hoped they would hit it off well. That certainly wasn't going to happen if Michael showed up with this sullen attitude.

Michael, Mia, and the kids arrived at six, just before the fast broke. The dining table at Hanaan's was laden with food. The sturdy wooden table seemed to strain under the weight of all the delicacies piled on top of it. Breads and meats, stews and salads, fruit and cakes all displayed on China dishes and glass platters.

"Hanaan, there is more food here than all of us could eat in a month."

Hanaan smiled. "My mother would scold me if she saw this. 'It's not enough for guests,' she would say."

"Arab hospitality." Mia smiled at Michael, trying to draw him into the conversation. He was staring at his shoes. *Fantastic.* She hoped no one else noticed how he was acting. Desperate to get the conversation going, she looked around the salon where they sat. "You have new curtains."

Hanaan grinned. "Yes, new curtains, some new furniture, and tomorrow we will get a new television. The end of Ramadan is coming. We must get ready for celebration."

Mia remembered the festivities of the previous year. All the accoutrements of Ramadan and the holiday that celebrated its completion reminded her of Christmas, in a secular way at any rate. Foods, clothes, gifts, and a general feeling of festivity alighted the atmosphere.

"Can we eat yet?" Dylan had spied a stack of *ta'meeya* on the edge of the table. Dylan found the pyramid of Sudanese-style hush puppies nearly irresistible.

"Not yet, sweetie. We have to wait for the announcement that the fast is over," Mia whispered, not wanting Hanaan to hear her. Their neighbor would surely let all the children eat first if she knew they wanted to. But that would go against Muslim custom, and Mia wanted to honor their way of doing things.

They sat quietly in the salon. Hanaan's husband made a few attempts at conversation, but there were long pauses in between the short spurts of conversation. Perhaps he was so hungry that he just wanted to eat. He was probably looking forward to the announcement more than Dylan.

"Tomorrow night is *Laylat alQadr*," he said, looking down at his lap and smoothing out his white *jallabeeya.*

"Yes, I've heard about that," Michael replied. "It's the twenty-seventh night of Ramadan, right?"

"Yes. It really could be one of several nights. We don't really know for sure. We have to seek Allah to find out."

Michael didn't respond. Mia looked over and saw him looking at his shoes again. She was getting agitated now.

Finally the radio announced the official time to break the fast. Hanaan passed around a plate of dates and handed her husband a glass of water to drink. Mia sensed the relief in Hanaan's family.

Once the dates and water had been served, Hanaan invited everyone to the table, handing out ornate China plates, even to the children. Mia eyed Dylan. *Great, just what he needs, a China plate.*

The man of the house was much more talkative after getting some food in his belly. Even Michael's mood seemed to lighten up. The atmosphere changed from politely quiet to a convivial house party with pleasant chatting and laughing. The children enjoyed themselves, trying out new foods and afterward, playing games with Hanaan's youngest son Saleh.

After a couple of hours, Michael looked at Mia and raised his eyebrows. It was *the look.* They had developed this silent communication to let each other know when it was time to leave. Mia returned the signal. After a few moments Michael thanked the family profusely for their hospitality.

"Oh, don't leave yet, it is still early," Hanaan's husband said.

This was the normal response in Sudan, even when everyone knew it really was time to leave.

"We have to get the children ready for school tomorrow," Michael said.

"All schools are closed for Ramadan," the man countered.

"The school opens late this month, but it is still open." Michael turned to the children. "Time to leave, kids."

"Leave? Already?" Corey asked, not taking his eyes away from the television.

"Yes, Corey, come on, time to go."

"Yes, sir." Corey turned to Saleh and said, "*Shukran.* Thank you."

Mia loved to hear her kids speak Arabic. They didn't know much, but she was proud when they used what words they did know.

"*Masha' Allah*, your son is getting so good at Arabic. He would make a good Muslim," Hanaan laughed knowingly. It was no use trying to talk Michael and Mia into becoming Muslim. In the same way, Mia wondered if it was any use trying to convince Hanaan to be a Christian. She was so content with life, she didn't seem to need anything, much less be looking for anything. "Oh, Mia, I am getting henna done tomorrow here at my house, you know, for *Eid al-Fitr*. Would you like to come get henna as well?"

"That would be great. What time?"

"Just come after the kids go to school. It's their last day before the holiday, right?"

"That's right. I'll see you around 10:30."

✳✳✳✳

"I found out who turned in the police report." Michael said, as Mia entered the bedroom. He sat on the bed with a serious look on his face. Mia had just told the kids good night and was hoping to enjoy a cup of tea before getting ready for bed. Michael's demeanor, however, had irked her all evening. Now she knew why he'd been so distracted. "Who?"

"Magid . . . one of the guys who does a lot of the paperwork for us at the office. I saw a typed report on his desk. I guess he left it there by mistake. I couldn't decipher it all since it was in Arabic. But I did see my name and the organization's name, and I did see that it said 'Report #8.' I think he's been feeding information to the police."

"Is this what was bothering you all evening?"

"Yes. I'm sorry I wasn't friendlier with Hanaan and her husband." Michael took off his shoes.

"What are you going to do?" Mia was sitting on the edge of the bed, watching her husband rummage through a laundry basket of clothes Tzega had folded earlier that day.

"There is not much I can do."

"Remember that part in Acts where Peter and John had been threatened, and they didn't know what to do?"

Michael reached for his Bible that sat on the nightstand and opened it to Acts. Mia had never imagined they would rely so much—literally—on

168

the words of this ancient text. She was beginning to understand what people meant when they called it the "Living Word."

"Now, Lord," Michael's finger followed the words of chapter four as he read, starting in verse 29, "consider their threats and enable your servants to speak your word with great boldness." He looked up at Mia. "Is that the verse you were talking about?"

Mia nodded. "Peter and John and the other believers didn't know what to do either. They just prayed and kept sharing."

Michael was thoughtful when he closed the Bible. "I think we need to pray and just keep telling others about Jesus. That's what the disciples did."

"Should we tell our family back home about any of these things that have happened recently? You know, so they can be praying for us?"

"I don't know, Mia . . . No, I don't think so. I know they want to pray for us, but some of the things that happen here are so far out of context for them. They would worry."

Mia knew he was right. She hated to keep secrets, though.

Despite knowing about the police report, Mia slept peacefully. She trusted that God had the situation under control. And it was more than just words—more than just a pat on the shoulder and a "God's got this" kind of peace. This was a true surrender. A devoted trust that she'd never experienced before coming to Sudan.

⇝ Chapter 30 ⇜

Rania dismounted the bus, carefully navigating its broken metal step. On the main street, before turning down her own, she stopped at a shop to buy a kilo of tomatoes. Not exactly what Father would expect she'd traveled all the way to the market to buy, but at least she wouldn't be coming home empty-handed.

Her heart felt lighter than it had in several weeks. Tonight she would figure out the truth and, *insha' Allah*, she would find true peace. The thought made her want to sing. But what to sing? She didn't know that many songs. She certainly wasn't going to sing Maysoon's songs or the songlike chants broadcast from Father's favorite Islamic radio. She wished she could remember the song she'd heard Halimah sing so long ago.

She remembered the event vividly. Halimah sang something about "heaven for eternity." The words and the tune were the most beautiful thing Rania had ever heard. She listened quietly for a minute, and then she told Halimah how beautiful it was. Halimah jumped, she remembered—as if she were startled, but even more than that. It was as if she were scared. When Rania asked her to sing it again, Halimah refused. She sang a silly song instead—a childish song that Haboba used to sing to them when they were very young. Rania had wanted to hear the beautiful song again.

As she made her way down the street in front of her house, Rania saw several men and boys from the neighborhood making their way to the mosque on the far end of the street. *Iftaar* was an hour away, they were probably headed to the mosque to get a good spot on the mats that were spread out across the street in front of the mosque. Tonight the men would eat together in front of the mosque, and many of them would stay at the mosque all night for *itikaf* to pray and read the Qur'an throughout *Laylat alQadr*. Father would be there—and Abdu, of course. He was more religious than all of her family members put together. Ali would go too. He was learning to be a man.

The men and boys, all dressed in white *jallabeeyas*, looked like clones walking down the street. But one figure caught her eye. He stood taller than most of the men. Even from the back, Rania could see his broad shoulders holding the folds of his pristine white *jallabeeya* like a stiff hanger. Jamal was so handsome. If he believed in *Isa*, why was he going to the mosque? Why was he filling his head with the Qur'an if he believed the Christian books were the truth?

She turned her head away and forced the thoughts out of her mind. It didn't matter. Tonight she would find the truth for herself. Tonight Allah would send her a sign. He had to. She had no other plan. This one had to work.

⁕⁕⁕⁕⁕

The three men of her house were walking out of the gate as Rania walked up. Father had piled a lofty turban on top of his head and looked very regal in his crisp *jallabeeya*. Rania had spent several hours that morning ironing the men's *jallabeeyas* so that not a wrinkle could be seen. Abdu looked just as regal as his father. Both men were tall and dark skinned with penetrating eyes and an air of confidence, something Rania had not inherited.

Abdu wore a *tageeya* instead of a turban. His headgear was a tight-fitting white rimless hat with swirls embroidered along the edges. Ali was stocky like Mama. His *jallabeeya* ballooned out to cover his belly that should not have looked so full on a day when he had been fasting. His eyes were solemn today, not mischievous like they usually were. He probably felt very important to be included in the observance of *itikaf* tonight. Any good Muslim would.

Rania hoped her bag of tomatoes was enough to fool her father. She needn't have worried, though, because his mind was on the evening's events.

"Got what you needed at the *souq*?" He asked. But he didn't even look at the bag.

"Yes, thank you."

"I asked Auntie Fareeda to come stay with you tonight," Father said. As he finished the words, Uncle Asim stepped out of their gate. He too was clad in the traditional robe and a white turban like Father's.

Rania hid her disappointment. "Thank you, Father. May Allah bless you tonight."

"And you as well, *habeebtee*." And with that, the men walked off toward the mosque.

Rania stepped inside the gate and pushed it shut. She had been hoping that she could be alone tonight. How was she going to get a sign from Allah if Auntie Fareeda was here? If she told her that she wanted to stay up all night and pray, her aunt would do it too. But if they both went to sleep, Rania would miss the Night of Power.

Rania followed the sound of clanking dishes and found Auntie Fareeda in the kitchen cooking. She wore a small scarf that covered her head and knotted neatly at the nape of her neck. The leopard print of the scarf clashed sharply with the pastel floral muumuu that she wore, but it didn't matter since they were home alone. Auntie Fareeda had skin like a smooth latte. A large latte. Like a good Sudanese Arab woman, she had grown several sizes wider within the first year of marriage. Sudanese men liked their women big. That being the case, Auntie Fareeda was quite the catch.

She had married Mama's brother, Uncle Asim, when Rania was too young to remember. Bashir was born nine months later. At first everyone was elated. A boy was born. *Masha' Allah*. The village where they lived celebrated this blessing from Allah. It wasn't very long, though, until the family realized that Bashir wasn't normal. He did not crawl when other babies his age were crawling. He did not talk when other babies were learning their first words. He eventually did, but much later. There were other signs too. Nothing that anyone could really point to exactly. But Bashir was different. When he was a teenager, his oddities grew more noticeable, and his parents determined that he had been possessed by a demon. They sent him to a *khalwa*, an Islamic school, hoping that the *sheikhs* there could help him. When they could not, Uncle Asim never went back to retrieve his boy.

"It's better for him," Uncle Asim said. But Rania did not believe it. Whether Bashir was the reason they only had one child, Rania didn't know. But she felt sorry for Auntie Fareeda. She was a beautiful woman and a good wife. She bore her husband a son, *Masha' Allah*. But that wasn't enough. She only had the one son, and he was not normal. All that was left was to be a good Muslim. Auntie Fareeda seemed to pour herself into that role with determination.

Rania remembered how Haboba talked about her children. When she spoke of Mama she would say, *"Masha' Allah*. Look at her successful husband. Look at her beautiful children." When she spoke of Uncle Asim, she would say, "You should look for a second wife. You know that Islam allows that." When Uncle Asim refused, Haboba would say, "Well, Fareeda is a good Muslim, *Masha' Allah*."

"I am making food for you and me." Auntie Fareeda smiled at Rania, who stood in the doorway. "Today we'll be celebrating *iftaar* together. It will be simple, but it will be delicious. Anything is delicious after fasting all day. Where have you been anyway?"

"At the market," Rania lied. She held up her bag of tomatoes.

"That's a long way to go for tomatoes." Auntie Fareeda stopped her bustling about and stared at Rania curiously. Then she shrugged and continued working. "You can cut them up, and we'll make a salad."

Rania washed the tomatoes in the sink and began dicing them.

"Auntie, do you think tonight is truly *Laylat alQadr*? Or do you think it was one of the other nights?"

"Oh, it is definitely tonight. This is the night Mohammed, peace be upon him, was transferred from Mecca to Jerusalem and met all the prophets in Al Aksa Mosque where they all prayed, and Mohammed, peace be upon him, was the *imam*, praying in the front with all the other prophets praying behind him. And then he was taken into heaven, to the top level, past where Gabriel could go. *Masha' Allah*, it was one-and-a-half meters from Allah."

What in the world was Auntie talking about? Rania wanted to ask, but the lady was on a roll. She obviously loved Islam so much and was geared up to teach Rania a few things. It was going to be a long evening.

"The Qur'an is a miracle you know, Rania. It is written in such high Arabic that even we who speak Arabic cannot fully understand it. Ah, but

Arabic is the language of Allah."

"Have you ever read the Christian books?" Rania knew it was a risky question, but surely Auntie Fareeda wouldn't tattletale on her.

"Oh, no, Rania. The Christian holy book was corrupted. It can't be trusted. The real one said that there would be a prophet after *Isa* whose name was Ahmed. But the Jews knew that, so they took that verse out. Now it is corrupted and we can't read it."

"Are you sure about that? How would you know unless you saw yourself?"

Auntie Fareeda stirred the stew thoughtfully. "We have to trust the *sheikhs* at the mosque, Rania. We can't fill our heads with questions."

Rania shrugged. "I can't help it. It seems like Allah wouldn't allow a holy book to be corrupted like that. Isn't He most powerful?"

"If your heart is right when you die, Rania, Allah will be merciful and let you into paradise. Your uncle is so excited about paradise. He says that in paradise there is a river of wine that you can drink from since on earth it is forbidden. And the wine won't have any bad side effects."

Where does Auntie get all this stuff? Why doesn't she try to find things out on her own? She sounds like a parrot, repeating everything she hears.

The women cooked until they heard the call to prayer from the mosque. Then they sat at the kitchen table and ate stew and bread and tomato salad in silence. Rania didn't feel like talking any more. She didn't want to hear Auntie regurgitating more stories about Islam. Half of them weren't true anyway. They were disjointed tidbits and random stories she'd heard other people say.

After washing the dishes, Rania watched television with her aunt. She hated watching Egyptian soap operas, but everyone else loved them. Auntie Fareeda was like everyone else. She sipped a small glass of steaming tea, eyes glued to the screen. Rania sipped her own glass of tea, trying to look occupied with the storyline although it wasn't interesting to her.

After three of the longest hours Rania ever remembered enduring, Auntie announced that she was going to bed. "You should sleep too, Rania. We'll be getting up early to eat before dawn."

"I will come soon, Auntie. I'm going to wash these tea glasses and tidy up a bit first."

Rania cleaned the kitchen, washed the tea glasses, swept the salon, and basically puttered around the house doing odd jobs here and there. At midnight she tiptoed to her bedroom and slowly opened the door. The light was off, but she could see the large form of Auntie lying in Halimah's bed. She heard the heavy breathing of a woman deep in sleep. Inhaling, exhaling, rhythmically and peacefully.

She crept across the room and quietly removed the small book from under her mattress. The bedframe creaked as she leaned against it. Rania froze and then wrinkled her nose and waited. Auntie snorted, rolled over, and started her heavy breathing again. Relieved, Rania tiptoed quickly to the door and shut it behind her.

She sat on the sofa in the salon where she had just spent three grueling hours with Auntie. She had about that many hours before Auntie awoke and they began cooking breakfast for the men who would be returning from the mosque at around four o'clock in the morning.

First, I need to pray. I need to ask Allah to give me a sign.

☙ Chapter 31 ❧

Rania knew no other way to pray than the way she'd done countless times since she was little. Midnight was not exactly the prescribed time to pray, but since it was *Laylat alQadr*, maybe Allah would make a concession tonight. She took a small rug and spread it on the floor in front of the sofa. The tip of the mat, the one with the gold tassel, faced east toward Mecca. Rania went to the bathroom and performed *wudhu*, the prescribed washing required by Muslims before prayer. Then she stood at the end of the mat opposite the gold tassel and greeted the angels on her shoulders.

"*Salaam aleykum*" over her right shoulder. "*Salaam aleykum*" over her left shoulder. Rania had been taught that everyone has an angel on each shoulder that writes down his or her good and bad deeds. On the last day, on *youm 'ilqiyaama*, there would be a scale to weigh the good and bad deeds. Even as she pictured the angels on her shoulders, Rania wondered: if Allah is merciful, what's the use of angels keeping track of my deeds?

After her prayer, Rania knelt on the rug, sitting on her feet and placing her hands, palms up, in her lap. She closed her eyes tightly and said, "Allah, if you sent *Isa* and He is the true way, please send me a sign. I think I believe in Him. Please, Allah, I want to find peace once and for all." Rania wrinkled her nose and thought for a few seconds before adding, "Even if it means leaving Islam."

After folding the prayer mat and placing it over the back of her father's favorite chair, she sat on the sofa and opened the book. "Now this is eternal life: that they know you, the only true God, and Jesus Christ, whom you have sent" (John 17:3). She continued to read the prayer that *Isa* prayed for His disciples. How wonderful it must have been to have *Isa* love them so dearly. In fact, the whole book was filled with love. These men were special to *Isa* and protected by Him. Rania wanted to be one of them; one of *Isa's* disciples.

She continued to read. "My prayer is not for them alone. I pray also for those who will believe in me through their message, that all of them may be one, Father, just as you are in me and I am in you. May they also be in us so that the world may believe that you have sent me" (John 17:20–21).

Could this be me? Could I be one of the ones Isa *was praying for?* The thought was almost too good to be true. But if it were true, Rania had no doubt this was the peace she had been looking for.

She couldn't stop reading now. She turned the pages with eager anticipation, as if she were reading the book for the first time. She'd read it before but, somehow, this time the words seemed clear.

Isa was betrayed by one of His close friends. One of His disciples. Righteous anger and aching sadness filled Rania's chest. And then there was the chapter in which *Isa* was killed. She'd always been told that *Isa* had not really died but rather His body was switched out with Judas the betrayer just before death.

But right here it says Isa *really did die. This story makes more sense.*

She went on to read the following chapter, and the sadness and anger left her as she read the account of *Isa* rising from the dead and appearing to His disciples. Her finger traced over the words, "Jesus performed many other signs in the presence of his disciples, which are not recorded in this book. But these are written that you may believe that Jesus is the Messiah, the Son of God, and that by believing you may have life in his name" (John 20:30–31).

Is it true? Are these words recorded so I can have life believing in Isa?

Rania leaned her head back and closed her eyes. She rehearsed the story she had just read. She imagined *Isa* dying after praying such a lovely prayer for His followers. She imagined His friends mourning. A peace filled her heart as she imagined *Isa* rising from the dead. Then she lay down on the sofa, head propped on a pillow, and fell asleep with a smile on her face.

The sun blazed through the window and the front door, which was inexplicably standing wide open. Rania sat up and rubbed her eyes. She must have fallen asleep on the couch.

The time was obviously well past four o'clock in the morning, which meant she'd somehow missed cooking and eating with her family. Where was Auntie Fareeda and where were her father and brothers?

She looked toward the open door again and realized it was not the sun shining through. No, the light was much too bright to be the sun. Her eyes stung and she squinted. Something shifted in the doorway and she saw a figure that was brighter, if that were even possible, than the light she had already seen.

A man in a white robe stepped toward her. Rania needed no introduction. She knew it was *Isa*. He held His hand out toward her, and she smiled and held her hand out to Him. As her fingers touched His, a sense of peace rushed through her veins.

Then He was gone, and so was the light.

BEEP. BEEP. BEEP.

Startled, Rania opened her eyes. She was still lying on the sofa in the salon. She looked at the front door. It was closed. She had been dreaming. She grabbed her cell phone sitting on the side table and looked at the time. It was 3:30 in the morning, and a message sign was blinking on the screen.

Still disoriented and feeling dizzy from the lack of sleep, she forced herself to sit up and check the message. Her heart skipped. It was a message from Halimah.

It is me. Can I call you?

Rania quickly tapped on the buttons and sent a message.

Yes.

Then she put her phone on silent so as not to wake Auntie, and waited.

In a matter of seconds—that seemed like an eternity—the phone vibrated in her hand. Rania nearly dropped it in her effort to answer quickly.

"Hello?"

"Rania? This is Halimah."

"Halimah." The name, forbidden to cross her lips, came out immediately followed by a quiet sob. Feelings Rania could not even describe filled her heart and mind. With hardly an introduction, she spilled out to her sister all that had just happened to her. She told Halimah about reading the book, about longing for peace, and about asking Allah for a sign. Then she told her about the dream she'd just had, followed by the message on the phone. "I think it is a sign, Halimah. I want to follow *Isa*."

Halimah's voice was like music from angels. The sisters talked until Rania knew that Auntie would wake up to begin cooking. But before they hung up, Halimah said they should pray together.

"How can we pray over the phone?" Rania asked, eyeing the prayer mat on the chair.

"God can hear us without washing our hands and feet and without kneeling on a mat, Rania. *Isa* said that we can worship Him in spirit and truth. We don't need to face a certain direction or do certain actions to be heard."

So, together the girls prayed, and Rania said out loud for the very first time that she truly believed *Isa* was the Son of God and asked Him to forgive her for all of her sins.

And then it was there. That peace. *Salaam*. The thing she had written on the dirty window of the bus. What she had been watching her friends search for. What she herself had asked for and hoped to receive. It was there. In her heart.

As Rania hung up the phone, she heard the heavy steps of Auntie Fareeda walking down the hall. Time to return the book to its hiding place. Time to cook. The men would be home soon, to eat before sunrise. Another day of fasting was about to begin. Mama would be home in a few days, and everything would be back to normal. Except nothing would be the same again.

≈ Chapter 32 ≈

Mia didn't like the Ramadan school schedule. By the time she got the kids to school and finished the needed chores around the house, it was about time to pick them up again. At least this was the last day. They would have a full week off for *Eid al-Fitr*, and then everything would go back to normal. Normal school schedule, normal work schedule. Normal. Unless they got kicked out of the country.

Either way, at least it won't be the Ramadan school schedule.

Mia arrived at Hanaan's house right at 10:30. As she rang the bell and waited for someone to open the front gate, she thought about her very first visit to Hanaan's. New in town, Mia was having trouble meeting Sudanese women. "They are never outside their homes," she lamented to Beth one day. Beth suggested they pray and ask God to make a way for her to meet her neighbors. The very next day Mia took a loaf of homemade banana bread next door and met Hanaan. Since then, some two years ago, Mia and Hanaan visited each other almost weekly.

Didi, the maid, opened the gate. "*Salaam aleykum.*"

"*Aleykum wassalaam.*" Mia shook Didi's hand. Hanaan stood smirking on the porch.

"You don't have to shake Didi's hand, Mia. She's just opening the gate."

"I shake your hand, don't I?" Mia was feeling courageous. Now, how could she transition to the subject of the gospel? She racked her brain for a Bible story about shaking hands but came up empty. So she just followed Hanaan inside.

"This is Fatima, she's going to do our henna." Hanaan motioned toward a young lady who sat on a short metal stool near the dining table. Hanaan smiled. "You want to shake her hand too?"

Mia looked at Fatima. Her hands were busy mixing the green henna powder with a black ink, so Mia just greeted her. "*Sabah 'ilxayr*, good morning."

"*Sabah 'innoor.*" Fatima returned the greeting robot-style. Then she turned to Hanaan and grinned. "*Masha' Allah*, she speaks Arabic."

"She is quite good, I agree. She is also learning to make Sudanese food. I taught her to make *aseeda*."

"*Masha' Allah*, she can make a*seeda*?"

Mia just smiled. She hadn't told Hanaan about the mess she'd made of her first try at the Sudanese food. Surely she'd get better at it.

As soon as she mixed the inky concoction, Fatima started work on Hanaan while Mia watched. She folded the henna paste into a plastic tube that resembled a miniature cake icing tube. Then she squeezed the henna into tiny lines and curls along the edges of Hanaan's feet and then her ankles. The designs were freehand and identical. That was quite a talent. After her feet and ankles, Fatima started in on the backs of Hanaan's hands.

When Hanaan's henna was done, she propped her legs on a stool to keep her feet from being touched by anything. She held her hands out in front of her, almost as if she were raising them in prayer. The henna paste would have to dry 20 or 30 minutes before she could rinse it off.

Fatima began working on Mia's feet. The sensation of the tiny lines of cold henna paste tickled, and Mia had to concentrate in order to not jerk her leg back.

"How much do you want?" Fatima asked.

"You should have henna all the way up your leg, Mia. Have you ever done that?"

"No, I've only done it on my feet."

Hanaan turned to Fatima, "Do it all the way up to her knees." Then she turned to Mia and winked. "Michael will love it."

Mia gave an awkward smile. After 45 minutes of intricate drawing, Mia looked at the finished product. It really was beautiful. She felt like a Sudanese bride getting ready for her wedding. Black flowers and tendrils swirled around her toes and chased each other all the way up her shins and calves. A matching design was drawn on her hands and arms. Because of the massive amount of henna, Mia was forced to balance awkwardly in her chair, attempting to keep her feet aloft and her hands up in the air.

This is Sudanese-style yoga.

While Mia maintained her balancing act, Hanaan disappeared to the bathroom to wash the paste off her hands and feet. When she returned, Mia examined her friend's skin. The black had stained her dark skin and left a beautiful design. Henna really was a lovely practice, Mia decided. There were lots of articles and warnings on the Internet regarding allergies to the black ink in Sudanese henna, but one could not deny its beauty.

Hanaan instructed Didi to bring tea for them, and she paid Fatima for her services and dismissed her. All the while Mia sat in an inelegant balance, concentrating on not letting anything bump her arms or legs.

"Hanaan, let me pay for my portion of the henna," Mia said from her precarious perch.

"Never," Hanaan exclaimed. "I invited you, so I will pay. It is our custom."

"Well, thank you. It is a very nice custom."

"Yes, Islam is beautiful. Muslims are very hospitable."

Mia didn't respond. What was she supposed to say? *Well, Christians are too?* That sounded a tad whiny. She prayed for wisdom. Then she decided that rather than arguing the point, she'd just go with it. Ask more questions. That might open Hanaan up.

"Speaking of Islam," Mia said. "I heard that tonight is a special night."

"Ah, yes, the Night of Power."

"Can you tell me about it?"

"*Laylat alQadr* is the night that Mohammed, peace be upon him, received the Holy Qur'an from the angel Gabriel. And on this night, if Muslims truly seek Allah, they can have all their previous sins forgiven."

"Wow, it would be wonderful to have your sins forgiven, huh?"

"*Masha' Allah*, yes."

"If you get your sins forgiven, say tonight, what happens if you sin tomorrow?"

"Allah is merciful. Here is our tea."

Hanaan busied herself instructing Didi on how much sugar to stir into the cups and correcting her with almost every move.

The tea was finally ready to drink, but Mia was still maintaining her balancing act. She was grateful when Hanaan looked at the clock and pronounced her henna dry.

"Didi, take Mia to the bathroom and help her rinse off the henna."

As Didi splashed water from the faucet onto Mia's legs and arms, she rubbed them gently to peel off the dried paste.

"Sometimes people have dreams," Didi said. She stopped rinsing for a moment and looked up at Mia. "During *Laylat alQadr*. Sometimes people have dreams from Allah, if they ask for a sign."

"Are you hoping for one?" Mia asked.

Didi grinned. "Of course."

"I will pray that you have a dream tonight. A dream about truth."

"Thank you."

"Didi," Hanaan called from the salon where she was lounging. "Are you almost done?"

"Yes, almost." Didi called.

Didi helped Mia dry off and then they examined the work. It was beautiful. The black against Mia's fair skin made the design stand out in stark contrast.

"*Masha' Allah*," Hanaan exclaimed as Mia returned to her friend. "Now you are a true Sudanese woman. Come, drink some tea."

Michael would bring the kids home at two, and Mia couldn't wait to show off her henna. In fact, she decided to wear shorts so he could see the full design that began at her toes and swirled up to her knees. Annie would be jealous and would want some henna of her own. Not that much of course. Perhaps she could find one of those little henna stickers for Annie to put on her hand.

At 2:15 Mia heard the car pull up and park outside the gate. That probably meant Michael was running late and would have to go right back to work after dropping off the kids. She swallowed her disappointment, knowing that he would get a full week of holiday after today.

The gate opened, and Mia stood on the veranda smiling. The kids came tumbling through the gate first. Giant grins were pasted across their faces—excitement that they were on a weeklong break. As they ran across the yard toward her, Mia looked to the gate to see Michael. After a few moments she saw a dark figure. It was . . . Habiib?

Habiib walked through the gate, laughing at the children. He also had a big grin on his face . . . until he looked from the children up to Mia, standing on the veranda in shorts, henna scrawled up her legs and arms. He froze. Even his smile froze across his face.

Mia froze too. She should have run away. Actually, she should never have been standing on the veranda in shorts in the first place. This was like being caught in your underwear. But the horror of it all immobilized her, and she stood like a stone statue.

Habiib attempted to gather his wits. "Mia . . . you are very . . . short."

Run away, Mia. Get out of sight. But she still just stood there. Perhaps he was referring to her shorts. His English wasn't that great.

Then, like a scene from a movie where the shot is frozen and then starts up again, Mia jumped into action. She smiled and said, "Thank you," though she still wasn't sure what his comment meant. Then she turned and ran into the house.

A few minutes later, Michael walked into the bedroom and saw Mia sitting on the bed clutching a box of tissue.

"Hey, Mia . . . what are you doing here? Wow, that's a lot of henna."

"Michael, I am so embarrassed." Mia put her head in her hands.

"Why? It looks great. I mean, it's kind of a lot, but it looks really pretty."

"No. I mean I was standing out on the veranda to show you, but *he* came in first." She raised her head and whispered the word "he" as she gestured toward the door.

"Oh." Michael's eyebrows rose. "That's probably why he went back out and said he'd wait in the car."

"What is he doing here?" Mia's eyes brimmed with tears.

"He wanted to ask me some questions . . . some spiritual questions, I think. So pray for us. I'm pretty excited."

"Um, yeah, OK. But mostly I'll pray that he gets that visual out of his head."

Michael laughed. "Don't worry about it, Mia. You were in shorts . . .

long ones at that."

Didn't Michael understand? A Sudanese man never saw a woman's legs except for his wife's and all the "loose" women on TV (at least that's what they thought about TV stars). How was Habiib going to believe anything Michael said when his wife dressed like a loose woman?

Then again, why on earth was wearing midthigh shorts a bad thing? Mia's pendulum of emotions swung over to the other side. What kind of country forces women to cover up from head to toe in 120-degree heat? This had to be the craziest place on earth. Why did she have to feel sinful for simply wearing shorts? Well, and for having henna drawn all over her body like she was a sketchpad.

Michael, unfazed by Mia's inappropriate appearance, kissed her on the cheek. "I've got to get back to Habiib. Don't worry about it, no big deal." He turned and left. "See you soon," he called to the kids as he headed out the front door.

Mia slipped out of her shorts and donned a long skirt. Simultaneously horrified at her own behavior and at the cultural norms of Sudan. She would never, under any circumstances, wear shorts outside the house again.

⇒ Chapter 33 ⇐

Michael was not nearly so excited when he returned that evening. Corey had asked to watch a DVD since it was not a school night. Mia negotiated a deal with the three kids, miraculously getting them to agree on the same movie. Once she made popcorn and they were captured by the story, she and Michael relaxed in the plastic chairs on the veranda.

The temperature had dropped to the low 90s, and the fan overhead created a pleasant breeze. Mia had recovered from her embarrassing moment. *As long as I never in my whole life have to see Habiib again.*

"So, I had an opportunity to share some deep stuff with Habiib. I told him my own story of how I came to believe in Jesus. I even told him how he could receive salvation, forgiveness for all his sins, hope for eternal life—the whole bit."

"Wow, Michael, that's amazing. . . . You don't seem happy about it."

"Oh, I am. It's just that Habiib also told me that Magid, the guy who is talking to secret police, is causing a lot of problems. I mean, he's turning in those reports, but he's also making up stuff. Kellar Hope is in real danger. No one can talk to Magid about it because whatever we tell him, he will take straight to the police. Habiib says that Magid is driving a brand new car. We all know he can't buy a car on the salary he gets from Kellar Hope. It's obvious the police are paying him. Habiib thinks our days here are numbered."

"Kellar Hope does nothing but help the people of Sudan. Why would the government want to close it down?"

"I think they just want all our stuff, you know . . . the computers, vehicles, a safe with a bunch of cash in it. Also, it seems like they don't really care all that much about their people. Especially the refugees, the ones we are helping."

"What did Habiib say about what you shared—your salvation story?"

"He is really interested. He wants to hear more. He even mentioned that maybe we could read the Bible together. I can hardly believe it was that easy."

"You must be much better at sharing about Jesus than me."

"No, that's the thing. I felt like I was stumbling through the whole thing, but he just kept asking questions. I know for sure that it wasn't any sort of skill of my own. Hey, tonight is the Night of Power. There are a lot of people asking for and looking for signs tonight. We should pray for them. I've heard that many times Jesus appears in the dreams of Muslims who are open to truth. Let's pray that will happen tonight."

The next day was Friday, but Mia couldn't sleep in. Her mind bounced from wondering if Magid would be successful in shutting down Michael's office to thinking about the Night of Power and imagining what would happen if Hanaan had a dream about Jesus.

Michael had promised to spend time with the kids, and he did, playing board games and hide-and-seek with the children all morning. He even allowed Mia a free pass on the latter, since she had to cook lunch.

Rest time for the kids after lunch was a nonnegotiable. Corey and Annie didn't take a nap anymore, but all three kids were required to spend an hour on their beds. They could sleep, read, or play a game quietly, but getting out of bed was not allowed. It was one of Mia's favorite times of day.

She'd hoped to spend the hour reading a new magazine Beth gave her, fresh from the United States—only a month old. She hadn't read one so recent in over a year.

When the kids were settled in their room, she combined milk, instant coffee, sugar, and ice into the blender to make an iced coffee. She poured the frothy mixture into a large cup and then settled on the veranda to relax.

The sweltering air all but melted Mia's skin. The thermometer said 110 degrees. The fan only served to blow hot air against her. But it was hot no matter where she sat, and at least outside there was also a breeze. As she opened the magazine and began to peruse the first page, Michael walked out and stood beside her. He looked like he was contemplating whether to say something or not.

She looked up at him.

"Well, we got some weird news. Good news . . . I think."

"What are you talking about?"

"Habiib called."

Mia cringed a little at his name. Thanks to him she was wearing the longest skirt she owned today. It even dragged the floor a little, carrying dirt with her where ever she walked.

"What did he say? Remember, our phones might be bugged."

"Well, about that, I don't hear any crackling or anything weird on it."

"Maybe they stopped listening in." Mia flipped to the next page of the magazine and examined the glitzy movie star that filled the entire spread. She took a sip of coffee. She was kicked back—leisurely talking about the phone being tapped by the secret police of an Islamic State. Sip, flip to the next page.

"Maybe." He pulled up a chair and sat facing her. "But here's the weird news. Habiib said that Magid has malaria, and this morning his family decided to take him back to his home village up north somewhere. He will not recover anytime soon, so his family sent his resignation to Kellar Hope and took him away this morning."

Mia suddenly realized she hadn't seen the mystery man on the street in the past day or two either.

⇒ Chapter 34 ⇐

If an outsider were to peek in the window of Rania's house, they would see nothing different than any other Sudanese Arab family. The men were religiously pious and die-hard soccer fans while the women were chubby and beautiful, scurrying about the kitchen and spreading the latest gossip. There were two differences, however. One was that Rania was a different person: a new person. No one else noticed . . . yet. But her new heart made all the difference in her outlook on life. The other difference was that, until now, Rania was still the only woman in the house.

Mama had not returned. The day after the night that changed Rania forever, Haboba died. Mama called on the house phone. Father said they could not make it to the *bika*, funeral, because of *Eid al-Fitr*. Rania begged to be allowed to go to Medani with Uncle Asim and Auntie Fareeda, but Father said she must stay in Khartoum.

So Rania and the men of her family spent the three days of celebration with Father's family across town. He had four brothers and two sisters. They were all loud and bossy. Rania did not enjoy visiting Father's side of the family. But at least their noise drowned out the sadness that nagged at her heart.

"Everyone smiles and laughs and eats," Rania told Halimah when she found time alone to call. "But on the inside no one is happy."

"What about Father? How is he?"

"Father said that it was Allah's will that Haboba died. But you know that's what every Muslim says every time something bad happens."

Rania couldn't help but wonder what surprise must have waited Haboba when she stepped into eternity and found that *Isa* was the true way, not Mohammed. The sadness that enveloped her heart also planted in her a strong desire to share the truth with her family.

⁂

When *Eid al-Fitr* was over, Mama returned home. She was different. She seemed to have softened since losing Haboba. Had she lost some fire in her heart? Or was she more affectionate toward Rania because she didn't want to lose another loved one? Somehow she seemed to see Rania, to listen to her more. Rania hated to have lost Haboba, but she liked the new attitude Mama possessed.

The joy Rania felt from her new heart full of peace and her deepening relationship with Mama was diminished by only one thing—Father's new obsession: a husband for Rania.

Father wanted Rania to marry Waliid, a distant cousin. His *zibeeb* was extra dark because he was ultrapious for the month of Ramadan. His giant smile was striking at first, but upon further examination, Rania predicted it would become decidedly annoying.

Waliid was tall like Jamal and looked regal in a *jallabeeya*. He had been at the *Eid al-Fitr* celebrations, and Rania had to admit to herself that she was somewhat attracted to him. When he led the men in prayers, though, and when he closed his eyes and quoted the Qur'an from memory, her skin crawled. How could she marry such a devout Muslim when she believed in *Isa*? Maybe Jamal could do it, but she could not.

Father was eager for a wedding, however. As soon as Ramadan and *Eid al-Fitr* were behind them, he began to talk over the phone with Waliid's father on a daily basis. He would raise his voice like all Arab men, and flail his arms about as they negotiated the bridal price. Rania wrinkled her nose. Mama beamed.

One day, a week after Ramadan, Father stood in the doorway of the kitchen where Mama and Rania were cooking.

"It is time to begin preparing for your wedding, Rania."

"What do you mean?" Rania looked up from the bowl of ground meat she had been rolling into meatballs.

"I mean that we have settled on a bride price, and Waliid's father is ready to make the engagement official." Father's eyes sparkled.

What was she supposed to feel? Weren't feelings just supposed to come on their own, without having to choose one and start it up yourself? Rania just felt numb.

"*Alhamdulillah*," Mama exclaimed.

"*Alhamdulillah*," Rania replied flatly.

⇒ Chapter 35 ⇐

The next day Rania slept late. She hadn't meant to. Mama, however, had kept her up late into the night chattering happily about wedding preparations.

Every Sudanese Arab girl dreamed about her wedding. Didn't girls all over the world do the same? The wedding celebrations were a girl's moment of glory—her chance to shine and be treated like a princess.

Rania had attended many weddings in her lifetime. She had also helped in the preparations for a fair number of weddings in her tight-knit neighborhood. The women bustled about for weeks gathering supplies of perfume and clothing and jewelry. The bride-to-be went into seclusion weeks before the wedding to undergo intense beauty treatments and memorize dances to be performed for all the women of the community and later for her husband only. The men discussed money and purchased presents and did whatever their wives told them to do in regard to renting a hall or paying for the honeymoon. It was a community affair and a very festive one.

Mama was beside herself with excitement, and Rania was excited too . . . sort of. This was the way of her people, right? It wasn't as though she had a choice, really. She needed to get married. Yet she wasn't quite sure what to do about being married to a Muslim while following *Isa*.

Even the men had gone to sleep when Mama and Rania finally turned out the last light and crawled into their beds. Rania was thankful she had nothing planned for the next day. It was Saturday, and since the weekend was Friday and Saturday, school wouldn't reopen until Sunday.

⬥⬥⬥⬥⬥

The sound of a cranky old rickshaw on the street outside woke her up. It wasn't that the motor of the three-wheeled vehicle was so loud as it was unusual that a rickshaw had navigated its way down her bumpy street. Why would a rickshaw be here?

Rania grabbed her phone from the bedside table and checked the time. It was already 11:00 in the morning. She got out of bed and smoothed the covers across her mattress. She tied a bandana-sized scarf around her head to tame her messy hair and peered out of her bedroom to see what was going on.

Mama was just walking in the front door and Rania could hear the old rickshaw driving away, its motor revving loudly. Mama juggled several large plastic bags. She looked like an oversized pack mule.

"Mama, what did you buy?"

"*Sabah 'ilxayr*, Rania. I've already been to the market while you have been acting lazy." Mama was grinning from ear to ear. "Come see what I bought."

Without waiting, she lugged her bags into the kitchen and then out a back door to a small open courtyard behind the house. This was the women's *hosh*, a small square of packed earth. High walls around the edges made it private. Many families had a private courtyard area for women, where they could cook, bathe, or perform beauty treatments without worrying about men showing up.

Mama put the bags on the ground and then dragged a low metal stool close so that she could sit and unpack her purchases. Rania watched as she removed a large clay pot, a plastic sack of charcoal, a large woolen blanket, and various bags and jars of woods, spices, and perfumes.

"*Dukhaan*," Mama said proudly as she surveyed her purchases.

"*Dukhaan*? Already?" Rania asked.

"It's a bit early just yet," her mother said, continuing to open bags and peer inside. "But I wanted to be prepared."

Dukhaan was a beauty treatment unique to Sudanese women, and therefore one that they were very proud of. "It not only smooths and tightens your skin," Mama said, "It is also useful for easing joint pain."

Mama took a broom made of long thin sticks and briskly swept an area at the back corner of the little courtyard. There was a hole about a foot deep in the ground. Mama took the new clay pot and set it inside so that it lined the hole. Then she emptied the bag of charcoal into the jar. Next she unrolled a giant round mat that had been stored in the corner and spread it out over the hole. The mat, tan-and-green stripes of woven palm branches, had a central hole that exposed the hole in the ground while covering the dirt around it. Next she placed a stool over the hole. The stool was a special one, built just for *dukhaan*.

Mama stepped back and surveyed her work proudly. "Now," she said, "I just need to buy the acacia wood and sandalwood to place on the coals, and you'll be ready for daily treatments of *dukhaan*."

She took the plastic bag holding the woolen blanket and hung it on a nail that protruded out of the wall. The blanket would be used to cover Rania's bare body as she sat over the smoking charcoal. She'd have to sit over the coals, fumigating her body with the musky scent for as long as her body could take the heat. Mama said once she got used to it, she would be able to do it for an hour at a time.

After treatments of *dukhaan*, her skin would turn orangey-brown. She would then rub her body with *dilka*, a homemade perfume. When she bathed, the residue of the *dukhaan* would be washed from her skin, leaving it smooth and emanating the undeniable scent of a Sudanese bride.

Rania admitted only to herself that she was nervous to sit over burning charcoal. A thousand possible mishaps popped into her mind. Haboba once knew a young woman who caught on fire when a burning charcoal lit her woolen blanket without her realizing it. Would that happen to Rania? She hoped Mama would stay with her in the courtyard the whole time she was sitting there.

Besides the fear of burning alive while trying to be beautiful, however, Rania was proud to be getting ready for *dukhaan*. It was a rite of passage, after all. She was becoming a woman. Father would be so proud. Mama would be so pleased. She was finally entering the world of adulthood. Rania had read enough magazines and watched enough television to know that *dukhaan* and *dilka* were practices that were unique to Sudan, and it made her proud to be Sudanese. She was going to be the most beautiful Sudanese bride, and she would make Waliid very proud to marry her.

Mama spent the rest of the day making *dilka*. This homemade perfume took several days to make, so Rania knew Mama would be obsessed with checking on it well into the coming week. She mixed together small bits of sandalwood, sugar, and perfume, among other things. She took all of these ingredients from the little bags and jars she brought home from the market. Next she began to work on a paste-like substance that would take several days to complete.

Rania sat on a stool across the courtyard from Mama and watched. She should have been observing the amounts of ingredients that Mama was mixing so that she would know how to make *dilka* once she was married. But she didn't. She watched Mama's face instead. Mama was focused, but her lips tipped up at the edges in a half grin. Surely Mama had wished she could have done all of this planning for her oldest daughter, Halimah. How devastated she must have been when she realized Halimah's wedding was never to be. Now, she had a second chance. Rania would get married. Rania was her only daughter now. This would be the only time that Mama would prepare a daughter for her wedding. Rania wanted to make her proud.

Suddenly Mama spoke, and her words took Rania's breath away. "Have you made any more drawings?"

Was Mama angry? Was she trying to catch Rania doing something bad? In fact, Rania had indeed made a new drawing. She had tried to capture her dream on paper. She'd tried to draw the shining window and the door with the glorious figure standing there. It was quite good, she thought, as far as drawings go. She was very happy with it in fact. But she hadn't shown it to anyone. Had Mama seen it?

"Yes." Rania replied.

"I'd like to see them. I think you have a talent for drawing."

Who are you, and where is Mama? Rania wanted to say. Since when did Mama care about anything that was different than Sudan and Sudanese culture? A girl learning to make *dilka* and learning to sit over burning coals: yes. A girl drawing pictures that come from her own thoughts and imagination: no.

"Thank you." Rania's voice was small.

Mama's hands were deep in the bowl of paste, and she looked almost as if she were playing with mud. She stopped kneading the mixture and looked right at Rania.

"Really, *habeebtee*, I mean it. You have a beautiful gift. I think you could be an artist."

Mama had always paid close attention to Halimah, but Rania had never felt her mother truly saw her, the younger daughter. Something had changed since Haboba died. Mama actually took the time to see Rania.

"I would like to study art, Mama. But I don't think Father will let me."

Mama looked back down at the mixture and began to knead again.

"Do you think Waliid will let me?" Rania's voice was filled with hope. Mama kept looking at the paste. She shook her head. "Mama, there is something else. It has nothing to do with marriage, or Ramadan, or *Laylat alQadr*."

"Rania, don't say it."

"But I have to. There is a way that we can be sure our sins are forgiven. We already lost Haboba, and I don't want to lose you. I want to tell you about *Isa*."

Mama's voice dropped to a whisper as she continued to work the *dilka* mash. "I know you have been reading the book."

"What book?" Rania's eyes were wide with surprise.

"The book, the one that Abdu did not find when he discovered Halimah's books."

"How did you know I was—"

"It doesn't matter. But Rania, don't speak of it."

"I want you to know about the peace I found."

"I am too old."

"What do you mean?"

"I am too old, Rania. I have my family, I have my traditions, I have my religion. I am too old to change. Go now, your father will be wanting tea. My hands are messy, so you'll need to heat the water."

"But—"

"Go." The word was spoken harshly, but when Mama looked up Rania saw that her eyes were glossy with unshed tears. "*Habeebtee*." She said in a soft voice. And as she smiled, a tear broke away and rolled down her cheek.

❧ Chapter 36 ❧

What a relief that Ramadan was over and the celebration of *Eid al-Fitr* was past. Mia didn't mind the holiday so much. They wore new clothes and spent two days visiting local friends, but the month of fasting was a true test of endurance, even for those who didn't fast during daylight hours.

Mia felt like Ramadan was often used as an excuse for laziness, traffic, bad driving, escalated emotions, and bad service. At least it was just one month out of the year.

Now that *Eid al-Fitr* was past, it was time to take action regarding Abbas's and Widad's request for baptism. Michael and Mia prayed for the full month of Ramadan about what to do with the Sudanese couple's request. Of course they should be baptized. But where in Khartoum would it be safe to do that? They had no tub, and the kids' splash pool was only 12 inches deep.

While eating yet another (of many) round of sweets during *Eid al-Fitr*, Michael and Abbas decided to arrange a trip to the Nile River.

"It could be like a picnic," Michael told Abbas. "We'll just take our two families out, and then while we are swimming, we'll baptize you. No one has to know that's what we are doing."

When Mia's family pulled up to Abbas and Widad's house early on a Friday morning, Yusra was standing outside smiling. She looked like she was going to a party. She wore her *Eid al-Fitr* dress—a frilly pink affair with blue ribbons and flowers across the hem and neckline. Abbas and Widad stepped out of their gate, and she saw that the couple was dressed equally as nice.

Mia felt the familiar slap of a culture faux pas. In contrast to the dressed-to-the-hilt Sudanese family, Mia had dressed her children—and herself—for an American-style picnic. The boys wore swimsuits and T-shirts. She thought she was being culturally sensitive by having Annie wear a casual skirt with shorts underneath. Her plan was to let her take the skirt off and swim in clothes that would cover her up more than a swimsuit. In her effort to appease the conservative side of the culture, she'd grossly missed the mark in regard to dressing up for the occasion.

Mia forced a smile and waved. She hoped that her long-sleeved T-shirt and denim skirt looked fancier than what it was.

The Sudanese friends, and recent brother and sister in Christ, hopped in the car, along with Yusra. Abbas sat in the front seat to help Michael navigate to a good picnic site on the edge of the Nile River. He said he knew a good place that he thought may not have as many visitors. This was a good idea because Friday was the national day off, and many families and groups would find their way to the banks of the river to spend the afternoon. They were counting on the fact that none of the Muslims, who made up 97 percent of the population, would picnic before Friday prayers at midday.

The waters of the Nile caught rays of the sun so that it sparkled like diamonds. The banks of the river were scattered with wiry acacia trees and littered with trash. The ground was too sandy for grass to grow in more than scattered clumps.

Abbas, Widad, and Yusra were unfazed by the unsightly beach. On the contrary, they acted more like children in a candy shop. Their eyes shone and all three sported grins. Mia realized that they probably had never done something like this before. They had no car and no extra money, and time away from the shop meant less money earned. In fact, Abbas had closed their little shop today, and only now did Mia stop to think of the financial burden that it placed on his family.

They unloaded a large woven mat and several baskets filled with bread, drinks, fruit, and sweets from the car. Mia and Widad unfolded the mat under one of the larger acacia trees and arranged the baskets on top. Mia proudly pulled out her platter of *aseeda*, formed perfectly just like Hanaan's. It turned out that *aseeda* was not that hard to make, it just took practice.

"Wear your shoes, kids," Mia called. "There are thorns all over the ground."

This, of course, was too late as Dylan had already stepped on a two-inch thorn that pierced the bottom of his foot. He shrieked in pain and started to cry. Annie ran to him and tried to pull the thorn out of his foot while he grabbed her for balance and continued to cry. Yusra, oblivious to the drama, ran for the water and Corey ran after her.

"Mom," he yelled. "She's headed for the water. She can't swim, can she?"

Pandemonium. Mia couldn't get away from it. Widad was busy smoothing out the picnic mat so Mia went to comfort Dylan while yelling in Arabic toward Yusra. "Let's don't swim yet, Yusra. Wait for the dads." She emphasized the last word, hoping the men would pick up on her hint.

In spite of her frustration, Mia was determined to persevere through today because it was baptism day. Even if it did her in, this was an important day, and she would do her part to make it happen.

After eating a snack, Michael told the Bible story of Jesus getting baptized. He was really doing well in Arabic. She hoped he thought the same when he listened to her speak. When the four kids began to fidget, Mia pulled out crayons and photocopies of a coloring page of Jesus she'd found. She congratulated herself for being prepared. It paid off, too, because the children were immediately appeased.

"It is important to be baptized like Jesus," Michael said, "because it is a step of obedience. When you are baptized, you are saying that you have chosen to follow Jesus 100 percent, and you are leaving your old life forever. Do you believe this? Are you willing to be baptized today?"

"Yes," Abbas said

"And what about you, Widad?" Michael asked.

"Yes," she said.

"Then this is what we will do," Michael said. "We will all go into the water. Mia will stay close to the bank with the children. Abbas and I will go a bit deeper. I will baptize Abbas. Then, Abbas, you baptize Widad."

Abbas looked at Widad and they both laughed nervously.

"Is that OK?" Michael asked.

"I don't know how to do that," the man replied. Widad just giggled.

"Just do what I do."

Mia thought about how back in Texas, they tended to do things without stopping to think of why. Take baptism. Only pastors or ordained men could baptize, right? When Michael and Mia looked it up in Scripture, they couldn't find any basis for that. If only pastors could baptize, what were people like Abbas and Widad supposed to do? They had read about Philip in the Book of Acts. He was a layperson. Actually, he was assigned to organize food for the widows in the church. He wasn't even one of the apostles or evangelists. But he baptized the Ethiopian in Acts chapter eight.

Wading out into the water, Yusra held up her frilly dress and squealed in delight. Dylan splashed Annie in the face, and she splashed him back. He had quickly forgotten about his thorn injury. Corey was more serious than the younger ones. He stood in the ankle deep water near the kids but watched as the men waded farther out into waist-high water.

Mia and Widad waded into the water. The muddy Nile water swished around her long denim skirt. She tried not to calculate how long it would take for denim to dry. What on earth was she thinking when she chose to wear denim? She'd obviously been thinking about the picnic and not about the baptism part. She looked back at the shore. No one else was picnicking just yet. She whispered a prayer of thanks. There was one group of young men throwing sticks into the water and laughing, but they were a hundred or so meters downstream and did not seem to be paying them any attention.

She looked back toward the men. They were waist deep now. Thankfully, the wind was blowing upstream so that their voices were not carried down to the stick throwers. Even so, Michael spoke softly so that she strained to hear his words.

"Abbas, you have said that you believe that Jesus is the Son of God and that He died, was buried, and came to life again to save you from sin. You have confessed that you want to repent from your sin and follow Jesus forever. Because of this I baptize you in the name of the Father, the Son, and the Holy Spirit."

The words were simple and quiet. The men didn't wear white robes, and Michael didn't raise his hand the way Mia saw her pastor in Texas do right before baptizing. He didn't even tip Abbas backward, was that OK? He simply held Abbas's hand for balance and helped him cover his nose and mouth. Abbas dipped down and the water covered him before he rose out, sopping wet.

A laugh rose from the little gathering downstream, and Mia glanced up quickly. But it was just the boys laughing about some shared joke. In fact, they were looking in the opposite direction. She looked back at Abbas. He was beaming.

Without hesitation, Widad waded out to meet her husband. Mia couldn't understand Abbas's Arabic as well as she could Michael's, but it sounded like he was attempting to repeat what Michael had said. Then he dunked his wife the same way Michael had done for him. She too beamed when she came out of the water.

"What are they doing?" Yusra was looking up at Mia. Mia wondered what her parents had told her about today. She wasn't even sure she knew the words in Arabic to explain to the little girl what was going on.

"Later, you can ask your mom, OK?" She smiled at the girl as she stood there holding up her frills with one hand and shading her eyes from the sun with the other. She looked baffled.

"*Mabrook*," Corey said with a giant smile as the three returned to the shallow water. "Congratulations."

The couple smiled. "*Shukran*," they both replied. "Thank you."

When they pulled away from Abbas and Widad's house after dropping the family off, Mia burst with the excitement she'd been holding in all day.

"That was amazing." She looked at Michael and saw that he was grinning too. "I can't believe you just baptized a Sudanese man. I never really imagined that this would happen."

"I know," he replied. "We pray for this all this time, but it's as though we never think it will actually happen."

Corey, eager to join the celebration, leaned toward the front seat. "It was awesome, Dad. You got to baptize. Do you think I will get to do that someday?"

"Maybe. You never know."

Contemplative, Corey leaned back. "I would like to."

Mia turned to the backseat to check on Annie and Dylan. They were fast asleep on either side of Corey. Wet from the water and dirty from the sand, Mia was half glad she had not put them in fancy clothes.

"I can hardly wait to tell Beth about this. Maybe we should have invited her."

"I don't know, Mia. Remember she gets a little worried when it comes to all this stuff."

"I know, but she is the one who gave Abbas a copy of the New Testament in the first place. Surely she would be glad about this."

"I think she's excited that they believe, but I don't know what she'd say about us baptizing them."

"It's biblical, Michael."

"I know. But Beth is trying to figure out how to share Jesus and also protect her job here. I guess sometimes you can't have both. That's why we make her nervous. She's afraid we'll jeopardize the job."

"Well, I'm going to tell her anyway. I think she'll be excited."

⇒ Chapter 37 ⇐

Beth came to the Westons' house on Saturday night. The kids were already in bed, and Mia anxiously awaited her arrival. Their friendship had been strained lately. But Mia hoped the news about Abbas and Widad would be well received. They had, after all, been together when Beth gave Abbas the New Testament. Mia hoped it would be a bonding moment—to mend their relationship.

The visit from her tall, regal friend, however, turned out to be far from friendship-building. Beth was stiff as she walked in. She sat in the salon with Michael and Mia, looking nervous.

"Let me go make us some tea," Mia said.

"No," Beth said. "I won't stay that long. I just wanted to tell you both that on Thursday I emailed the home office. I felt like Kellar Hope should know some things. I told them that against my advice and warnings from others, Michael has continued to share about Jesus with people both in and out of the office."

Mia's excitement quickly turned to anger toward her friend. How dare she? She, who was so worried about protecting their jobs, was now putting Michael's in jeopardy?

"I'm sorry to hear you did that," Michael said. His voice was calm.

"I'm sorry if it hurts you. I had to do what I thought was right."

"And we have to keep doing what we think is right."

Mia didn't say anything. She was stunned. So, this was what it felt like to be betrayed by a friend. She wanted to ask Beth why she hadn't come to them first. But she knew the answer already. She knew that Beth would say she had already tried to warn them. And honestly, maybe she had. It wouldn't have stopped them though. They were convinced that Acts was the answer to so many of their questions.

She recalled the verses they had read. "But Peter and John replied, 'Which is right in God's eyes: to listen to you, or to him? You be the judges! As for us, we cannot help speaking about what we have seen and heard'" (Acts 4:19–20).

She wanted to belt the Scripture out to her friend, but she was too angry to even speak. And she felt a pesky self-righteousness creeping up in her heart. She was definitely not in a good place to be flinging Scripture at anyone.

When Beth was gone, Michael and Mia locked the door and went to bed. In the dark, lying side by side in bed, Mia finally spoke.

"Do you think we were wrong? To be so bold, I mean."

"No."

"I don't either. Do you think you'll lose your job? You know, since Beth has insinuated that you are the one getting the office in trouble?"

"I don't know. I got an email tonight saying Dr. Kellar wants to have a conference call with me. I think it would be good for you to be there too."

"Oh, Dr. Kellar himself? Wow. We really are in trouble." They lay in silence for a few moments. "I feel like Beth betrayed us. I shared a lot of stuff with her. She's my closest friend here. I thought we had the same goals . . ."

"I know. I'm sorry. It's one thing to be hurt by an unbeliever. That's painful, but nothing like by being hurt by a fellow believer."

≈ Chapter 38 ≈

Mia's head ached when the alarm went off the next morning. A wadded-up tissue teetered on the edge of her bedside table, and when she reached over to turn off the alarm, she sent it careening to the floor. She turned to wake Michael, but he was already out of bed.

Mia rolled out of bed and headed to the kitchen. Michael was sitting at the kitchen table reading his Bible. He looked up and smiled wearily.

"Good morning, honey," Mia said.

"Good morning." Michael ran his hand through his black hair and watched Mia as she poured a cup of coffee, stirred in a heaping spoonful of creamer, and sat at the table across from him. "I didn't sleep much last night."

"I wondered. You look tired."

"Yeah, I was praying a lot. And reading the Bible. Remember this verse? First Corinthians 16:9 'a great door for effective work has opened to me, and there are many who oppose me.'"

Mia sipped her coffee. "Wow, I was thinking about opposition from Sudan. You know, unbelievers, the government, the police. Even the heat and the difficulty living here seem like opposition from a spiritual enemy. I hadn't once thought about the opposition coming from within."

"Well . . ." Michael took a swig of his own coffee. "We told each other that we believed God is sovereign over our work here and that He would take care of us when the police were hassling us. Now we have a new decision."

"Whether or not to trust God even with Beth's email and Dr. Kellar's conference call."

"Right. And I think we decided a long time ago. When we first moved to Sudan, we knew that's what we believed. I think this is where our actions will show we truly believe."

"So, we don't defend ourselves, we don't tell Dr. Kellar all the reasons we think Beth's email is wrong. And if he fires you, he fires you."

"It doesn't feel like a great door for effective work opening, does it?"

"Not until I remember the look on Abbas's face when he came up out of the water. Honey, if we had to leave tomorrow, I wouldn't regret a thing. It was totally worth it."

"Yeah, that's how I feel too. I just don't really want to get fired."

Mia reached across the table and grabbed Michael's hand. "I think we should pray before this day gets started." It sounded trite, she knew. But she also knew her husband, and he understood. Prayer was never trite.

⁂

"Mom, why are we watching a movie on a school day?" Annie asked. "You never let us do that."

"Well, today I am giving you a treat." Mia turned on the TV and put in the DVD.

"Is everything OK?" Corey asked.

"Yes, everything is fine. Dad and I just have an important conference call. We are going to be in the bedroom, and we need you guys to stay out here."

The time difference between Dallas, Texas, and Khartoum, Sudan, was eight hours. For Mia, it was four o'clock in the afternoon, but for Dr. Kellar, it was eight o'clock in the morning, the beginning of his workday. Mia had been praying all day that Michael would be calm and peaceful as he awaited the call. She imagined he was rehearsing several scenarios in his mind. Was he going to be reprimanded? Disciplined? Fired? Kellar Hope Foundation was run on Christian principles, but it was not a Christian organization. Did the others in the office know that Beth had notified Dr. Kellar? All Mia could do was pray and try not to grow angrier at her friend. Michael had made a makeshift office by setting up a card table and two chairs. He even hung a picture on the wall behind them.

"Wow, you really must have been worried about this meeting. You've never put this much work into an Internet conference call."

"I've never actually talked to Dr. Kellar before. Honestly, I'm pretty nervous."

"You're gonna be great." Mia hoped she sounded confident. It was ironic that Michael's chance to actually talk to the one-and-only Dr. Kellar—the founder of the foundation whose work they believed in—was the time that he was going to get reprimanded . . . or worse, fired.

At exactly four o'clock Michael's laptop began to ring. Michael sat up straight and pressed the *answer* button. It took a few seconds to get the audio and video adjusted, and it wasn't crystal clear. But sure enough, there was Dr. Kellar on the other end. Mia recognized him from the portrait that hung in the reception area of the home office back in Dallas. She and Michael had seen him from a distance a few times in the past at various conferences. They had actually met him once. But they had never had a conversation with him. This was the first. Maybe the last.

Dr. Kellar was a nice man. Mia let her shoulders relax as she listened to his deep voice. He asked Michael about work, about his experiences, and even asked his opinion on a few items particular to the Khartoum work. Then he brought up the pervading issue.

"So, Michael, I guess you know about the email Beth sent to me."

"I didn't read it, sir, but I know she sent one."

"I appreciate her concern and her honesty."

"I understand, sir."

"I have to tell you, I have been wanting to craft the foundation so that it can go beyond simple social and physical care. Up until now I have not figured out a way to do that, especially in places like Sudan."

Here it comes. The blow. At least he's being humane about it.

"I commend you and your wife for your courage."

Those were his words. Mia was sure of it. She heard them plain as day. But she could hardly believe it. She tried to pay attention as Dr. Kellar continued, but those words kept buzzing in her ear. Did he mean, "I *condemn* you and your wife"? No, that's not what he said. He definitely said *commend*.

The older gentleman continued talking. He talked about a new position back at the home office in Dallas that would head up a new evangelical strategy for the regional offices around the world.

"I think you are the man for the job, Michael," he said. "It is a better salary package, and it is a chance for you to bring your family back to

Texas. I know your wife's family lives nearby."

Even at the sound of those words—those words that she would have given anything to hear just a year or two before—Mia knew they couldn't. She reached across the desk and grabbed a note card Michael had written on. She tapped the card and looked at Michael. He nodded at her and grinned. The card read, "A great door for effective work has opened to me."

"Dr. Kellar, Mia and I have always been honored to be a part of Kellar Hope Foundation. I was honored to work at the home office for a number of years, and now we have grown to love living and working in the Khartoum office. I wholeheartedly support your idea to focus on evangelism as a part of what Kellar Hope can do in countries around the world. While I am happy to give thoughts or suggestions, I cannot take the job you have offered me. Mia and I believe very strongly that our time in Khartoum is not finished. We would like to stay here."

"Do you mean to tell me that after all the trouble and the threats you have endured, and with no guarantee of how long you can even stay there, you would still pass up this opportunity and continue your work in Sudan?" He paused. "You have a way out, you know. This is it."

"Yes, I know. I would love to be considered for the position after we finish our second contract here, if there is an opening."

"I cannot say with confidence whether there will be," Dr. Kellar said. "And furthermore, I cannot guarantee your safety in Khartoum. Things are getting pretty sticky."

"I understand that, Dr. Kellar . . . we understand that." Michael took Mia's hand and squeezed it. "But God is sovereign, sir. He brought us to Sudan, and we will stay here as long as He allows us to."

"Very well, then. I will look for someone else to fill that position. I will continue to pray for the work in Khartoum, both the official stuff and the unofficial." At this, the man winked. "And we will continue to monitor the political situation and pray for God's grace to allow you to stay there."

"Thank you, sir."

"You are very welcome. Keep up the good work."

⇒ Chapter 39 ⇐

I'm getting married," Rania whispered to Halimah over the phone. "When?"

"I don't know yet. Father should be arranging the date soon, though. I'm going to marry Waliid, our cousin. Do you think I can be a Muslim and a Christian at the same time? Jamal thinks so."

"Rania, the Bible says you cannot be unequally yoked. That means you cannot bind yourself to someone who does not believe in *Isa*."

Rania thought about those words over and over. Halimah was right. Her allegiance was now to *Isa*, and she could not tie herself deeper to a community that did not believe He was truly the Son of God. That's what Jamal had done, and she could no longer see any desire on his part to follow *Isa*.

She had, in fact, confronted Jamal about it just the day before, when he came to the front gate to bring a soccer magazine to Father. What was it with the men of the neighborhood anyway? Couldn't they buy their own copies? Why did they pass around one copy until it became old and tattered so that they had to tape the pages to keep them from falling apart?

Rania answered the gate and was startled to see him. He handed her the magazine, and she saw the henna stains on his knuckles and palms. They were left over from his wedding—it had been held two weeks after Ramadan finished. She tried not to feel disappointed. She was, after all, getting married herself.

"This is for your father," Jamal said. His gaze made Rania squirm. "You didn't come to my wedding."

"I was sick," she lied.

Jamal stuck his hand into the side pocket of his *jallabeeya* and retrieved a rectangular object wrapped in a white cloth. "This is for you."

"What is it?" Rania asked. Maybe a wedding gift?

"It's a Bible. It's all the Christian books in one."

A smile stretched Rania's face, though she tried to remain indifferent.

"I can't keep it at my house anymore."

"Oh, it's yours?"

"Well, it's yours now," Jamal said with a shrug.

"Do you not believe it anymore?"

"I still believe it. I just can't let anyone know."

"Then, what's the use believing it? What difference can it make in you if it doesn't make a difference in others?"

"Look, I tried talking about it. I even asked some questions to the *sheikh* at the mosque. It was nothing bad, I just asked a few questions to talk, you know, like a discussion."

"And?"

"And the next day three *sheikh*s came to my house. One of them offered to slit my throat."

Rania felt dizzy at the thought of hearing such a threat. Her hands shook as she took the book from his hands.

"I will keep it here for you," Rania said.

"I doubt I'll ask for it back," he replied with sadness in his voice. "I am married now. I have to think of the safety of my wife."

<hr />

The next day Rania shut herself in her room and spent the morning drawing. When she concentrated on hues and focused on shapes and designs, her heart settled and her mind cleared. She also unfolded the white cloth and read from the book Jamal gave her. She found that *Yohana*, the book she already had, was included in this larger book, along with many others. Her heart beat with excitement over this treasure. There was so much to read. So much yet to learn about *Isa* and this peace that He had put in her heart.

At noon she put away her drawing materials and hid the book. She started toward the kitchen to find something to eat, but on the way, a sparkle in the salon caught her eye.

She walked to the sitting area and found a beautiful golden tray overflowing with an arrangement of cosmetics and perfumes. The display was wrapped in clear cellophane and tied at the top with an elegant golden bow.

"*Shela*," Rania said.

"Yes, wedding gifts," Abdu said as he approached from behind. Rania turned at the sound of his voice and saw he was carrying a second tray festively wrapped in cellophane. "And here is another one."

Her brother set the tray on the salon table next to the first. The second one was smaller, but the arrangement stood taller. The shape of a three-dimensional heart, along with swirls and curls, rose about a foot from the tray. The shape was made entirely of crisp Sudanese bills, folded and rolled to create a beautiful display.

Rania and her brother admired it together. "This must have cost more than 2,000 Sudanese pounds."

"Really? Who is it from?"

"Uncle Asim and Auntie Fareeda."

"Isn't it early to be receiving *shela*?"

"Not anymore."

Abdu and Rania turned at the sound of Father's voice.

"What do you mean?" Rania asked.

"The date has been moved up. You'll be getting married in just over a month. We've signed the agreement, and Waliid should be sending gifts to you soon. They've already purchased clothes and jewelry for you."

Rania was stunned. "A month? Why so soon?"

Father sighed heavily. "Because this neighborhood has had enough bad news. We need something good to happen. A wedding will bring honor back to our neighborhood and our family."

Rania wasn't hungry anymore. She turned and ran back to her room, trying to hide her tears. A few minutes later, Mama knocked quietly on the door.

"Rania, it's Mama. Please let me in."

Sniffling, Rania unlocked the door for her mother. They sat in silence for a few minutes, Rania on her bed facing her mother, who sat on Halimah's bed.

"Did you know that Father moved the wedding up?"

"No, *habeebtee*, I only found out just now, when you did."

Rania sniffled. "Waliid is not a bad man, Mama. He will make a good husband. But I don't want to marry him."

"You will have to marry him, Rania. You are engaged. But . . ." Mama moved to Rania's side and stroked her hair. "Marriage is not for you right now. You have acquired the same spunky spirit your sister had."

Rania looked down at her lap, but her heart thumped. Mama had not mentioned Halimah in a year. "But I have to get married now, Father says so."

Mama sat quietly for several minutes and then spoke in a hushed tone. "I have an idea. Your father has a cousin who teaches at the American University in the Emirates."

"The Emirates?"

"In Dubai. I spoke with his wife, and she says you could live with them and possibly even attend the College of Fine Arts and Design."

"You mean leave Sudan? Father would never let me."

"Let me talk to your father. I can make a convincing argument to simply postpone the wedding."

"What about you, Mama? You want me to get married, don't you? I couldn't bear to disappoint you."

Mama smiled and cupped Rania's face in her two plump hands. "You have a gift, *habeebtee*. You are an artist. Plus, you have the same wandering heart that your sister had. Sudan is not safe for you. Sudan is only safe if you follow its rules. Yes, I want you to get married. But more than that, I want you to be safe."

Rania thought about Mama's words. Everything was right about what she said except for the part about a "wandering heart." Rania was confident that ever since she believed in *Isa* as the one true way to God, her heart had found its home and had stopped wandering. How she wished Mama would stop and read the words of the precious book. The words that were written, "that you may believe that Jesus is the Messiah, the Son of God, and that by believing you may have life in his name" (John 20:31).

"I would love to study in Dubai, Mama."

The older lady smiled. "Then stop worrying. I will talk to your father."

Rania wasn't so sure how easy that would be. Father was a kind man, but he had a temper. He would not take kindly to Mama changing his plans.

When Mama left the room, Rania fell to her knees and prayed. She did not grab a prayer mat, she did not perform *wudhu*, she simply poured her heart out to God and felt wonderful peace flood her veins.

✑ Chapter 40 ✑

Rania listened to her parents' voices coming out of the salon. She could have heard Father's tense voice all the way down the hall to her room even if she hadn't been eavesdropping.

"I know Rania is upset, and she wants you to talk me out of this. But I have made my decision. Rania must marry immediately. We have waited too long to regain the honor that was taken away from us."

Father was referring to Halimah's choice to follow Jesus and leave Islam.

"Yes, she must marry. You are a wise man," Mama said. "And we must do everything in our power to insure that she and Waliid have a strong foundation. Together they will give us a good name."

Father grunted his approval. Rania held her breath and waited, but her heart felt as if it was sinking. Mama had given in to Father's demands.

Then she heard her mother's voice again. It sounded soft and yet possessed an air of confidence.

"*Fee ilajla innadaama wa feetaanee issalaama*. In haste there is regret, but in patience and care there is peace and safety. That's what your cousin Faisal always says."

"Ah, Faisal, he is a good man. Very wise, that one. Don't forget to put him on the guest list."

"Oh, that would be wonderful if he could come, wouldn't it? I will most definitely invite him . . . although I doubt he will approve of your haste in moving the wedding date. It will be a shame, you know, that most of our wealthy relatives will not be in attendance."

At the word *shame* Rania could imagine her father bristle and sit up straight in his favorite chair.

"What do you mean?"

"Well," Mama said, "of course our relatives who live out of the country have very important jobs. They will not be able to honor us by making arrangements with such short notice. In fact, I know many of the women in the neighborhood are already talking about this wedding being the main event of the year. They will most certainly be inviting their out-of-town relatives as well. I am sure it will still be a wonderful wedding, even without the businessmen who will wish they could have attended."

"How much time do you think they need?"

Rania bit her lip and waited. Mama was patient and did not reply quickly.

"Well . . ." she drew out her answer as if trying to calculate. "Events as big as this, the wedding of your one-and-only daughter, they take time. It's not only the guests we need to think about. We must also make sure we can reserve the largest hall. You know a lot of influential people. They will all want to be notified so that they can attend."

"If we wait too long, Rania will get wild ideas in her head. She may do something . . . drastic."

Mama chuckled. "How did I get so lucky to marry such a wise man? You are most definitely right. It is not a good thing to have Rania here when we postpone the wedding. It would be very wise to send her to live with family far away. But . . . where could she go? Haboba is gone. Who could keep Rania for us while we plan the wedding? Who is wise enough to guide her—someone like Faisal, but of course it couldn't be him."

"Why not?" Father asked.

"Oh, no, that would never work. Faisal and his wife live in Dubai."

"Exactly." Rania could hear the salon chair scrape against the tile floor as her father stood in resolution. "That's exactly why she should go. Faisal will keep her out of trouble and away from the silly gossip of the ladies in our neighborhood. We will postpone the wedding until we are sure all my associates and all of our relatives can come. You are right, this is an important event."

"Very well. I will contact Faisal and ask if Rania can live with them. Perhaps he will find a school she could attend while she waits."

◆◆◆

Rania could hardly believe it was happening. She was moving to Dubai. She had been accepted to an art school. The *shela* had been returned, the marriage to Waliid had been postponed indefinitely.

As Rania selected her best clothes to pack in her small suitcase, she thought about the last conversation she had with Halimah. Her sister told her that the good news of *Isa* would spread because of cases like hers. She was right, of course. Several people in the neighborhood had learned about *Isa* because of Halimah. Mama knew, Rania knew, even Maysoon and Jamal. When Rania moved to Dubai, perhaps she would share with Faisal and his family. Even if it was slow, the news of *Isa* and the forgiveness and peace He brought was spreading.

Rania put the last of her belongings in the suitcase and closed it. The large book, the Bible, was wrapped in a *tarha* and placed under a Qur'an. She hoped no one at the airport would look below the Islamic book. Now it was time to say some good-byes.

Her first stop was Maysoon. They met at the cultural center. Mel was in her office there, and she told Rania how happy she was that Rania had the opportunity to pursue art. She wished her all the best.

"So, you're leaving this place before me, and I'm the one who wanted out of here." Maysoon smiled, but her words betrayed a hint of sadness. Rania had been right about Maysoon. Her attempt to live on her own did not work out, and she had moved back home with her family.

"I will pray that one day you will find your own way out. But more importantly, Maysoon, I will pray that you will find the truth that will bring peace to your restless heart. I don't think true freedom is what you think it is."

"I wouldn't mind hearing more about it, Rania. Maybe we can stay in touch."

"*Insha' Allah.*" Rania laughed and hugged her friend, kissing her on each cheek. "I already miss you, *mushtagiin.*"

"*Bilakthar.* I miss you more."

Rania had one more errand before leaving. Halimah had given her instructions on where to find the home of the foreigner from her encounter at the cultural center. She took a city bus and then walked two blocks from where it dropped her off. The houses along the streets of this neighborhood did not have numbers posted, but Rania found a white gate with blue trim, as Halimah said she would. She heard the sound of children playing in the yard just on the other side of the privacy wall, and their unfamiliar words confirmed that this was the house of a foreigner. Rania knocked on the gate and listened as footsteps shuffled toward her.

The gate opened, and there stood the lady who'd given her Halimah's number. Rania was relieved. She had not made a plan for what she would have done or how she would have explained herself if someone other than the lady had answered the door.

"*Salaam aleykum*," Rania said.

"*Aleykum wassalaam*," the lady replied. Her eyes widened with recognition and she smiled. "Come in." She opened the gate further to allow Rania to enter.

Rania looked over the lady's shoulder into the yard. She recognized the boy who had also been at the cultural center, and he was playing with two other children who must have been his siblings. Even from where she stood at the gate, Rania could sense that peace and joy filled this home. She almost agreed to enter, but she remembered that her parents were at her own home waiting on her.

"*Shukran*," Rania said. "But I cannot come in. I want to say thank you for giving me the phone number. It changed my life. Well, actually *Isa* changed my life." It felt good to say the words without fear of getting slapped or yelled at . . . or disowned or beaten or killed.

"I am so happy to hear that," the white woman said.

"I am moving away. But I wanted to give you something. I can't bring all my art pieces with me, so I want to give you this." Rania held out the wrapped package.

The lady raised her eyebrows. "*Shukran*." She looked pleased.

"You are welcome." Rania smiled. Then she looked at the time on her phone. "I have to go now. My family is taking me to the airport soon."

"*Allah ma'ik*, God go with you."

"*Allah yabarak feekee*, God bless you."

<hr />

Rania sat in the backseat of Father's old white sedan as they drove to the airport. Dubai was only one flight away. Father's cousin Faisal would meet her when she arrived. She would only be alone for a few hours, and even then she'd be surrounded by other Sudanese people on the plane. Rania repeated these things over and over to herself to keep her nerves at bay. This was her first time to leave the country.

Father and Abdu sat in the front seat. They were silent. Neither one was happy with the idea of Rania leaving, though Father had assured her that this was for the best. The one saving factor was that it did actually sound very wealthy and cosmopolitan to say that their daughter and sister was studying abroad. And the fact that Dubai was a Muslim country kept their reputation clean.

Mama, Ali, and Rania squished into the back seat. Ali looked sad and a little scared. His big eyes reminded her of how she felt when Halimah had walked out of their house that fateful morning so long ago.

Mama looked resolute. She had effectively convinced Father that he himself had come up with the plan of sending Rania to Dubai. She would miss Rania terribly, but a mother will do anything for her child. Rania had given her mother the small book that had changed her life. She made her promise to at least read it and also to let Ali read it. Mama had promised the first part, though she made no promises regarding Ali.

The airport was a visual cacophony of *jallabeeyas*, *tobes*, and piles of bulging bags pushed on metal carts. The frenzy of passengers arriving and leaving and family members calling and waving was disorienting. Before she knew it, Rania had hugged each member of her family goodbye and was standing in line at the check-in desk. Was this real? Was she really going to school in Dubai? Had *Isa* really proved Himself sovereign by making a way for her to believe in Him? It appeared to be the truth. When she pinched herself, she didn't wake up from a dream.

➤ Chapter 41 ➤

"What's that, Mommy?" Annie eyed the poster-sized package in Mia's hands.

"I don't know yet, Annie. A special lady gave it to me. Let's open it and see what it is." Mia ripped away the wrapping and pulled out a picture. The frame was typical for the region: simple, wooden, spray-painted gold with splinters waiting for unsuspecting fingers.

"It's pretty, Mommy." Annie smiled. "It's a door."

Mia shook her head in amazement. *A door.* Mia recognized the rectangular columns on both sides and the geometric shapes etched into the frame. The style was Nubian, very Sudanese. The colors were vibrant; the background and edges were dark. The typical double-door entrance looked as if it was cracked open just a bit. Golds and yellows, like bright light, spilled out and invited the onlooker to enter.

"A great door for effective work has opened to me, and there are many who oppose me."

"What does that mean, Mommy?"

Mia looked down at her daughter and smiled. "It means God is sovereign. It means He is in control. All the time." Looking back at the picture she tipped her head. The shadows made the colors vibrant and the jagged edges of the geometric shapes made the rounded edges appear smoother. The hard with the easy. The good with the bad. "It also means I need to do a few things to show God that I believe He is sovereign."

Annie tipped her head, and studied the picture. "It means all that?"

***

"It means I need to forgive Beth. And it also means I need to go find Lily, a beggar girl." Mia held the picture up proudly for Michael to see.

"It means all of that?" he asked, eyebrows raised.

"Ugh. You sound just like Annie." Mia's frustration crumbled into a laugh. She looked at the picture again. It was so obvious to her. "Yes, it means all that."

Mia stared across the table at Beth. She would not allow herself to be offended by Beth's rebuff of her dinner invitation. Perhaps meeting in a neutral place for tea was a better idea after all—even if it was Beth's idea.

Her friend perused the piece of paper that served as a menu. She was tall and beautiful, and dressed so stylish that even her ultraconservative clothes announced to everyone that she was sophisticated. Mia looked at her own wrinkly brown skirt and dowdy green blouse. No, she would not allow herself the luxury of jealousy.

"I'll take a caramel macchiato," Beth said to the young waitress who scribbled it on a notepad.

"I'll take hot tea, please," Mia said.

"So, in light of the likelihood that Kellar will be closed down anyway in the near future, I have accepted a transfer to the office in Casablanca. They are in desperate need of a nurse there, and I think it will be a good fit for me."

Casablanca. The name alone has sophistication written all over it.

"Good for you." Mia forced herself to smile.

"This job is a promotion. Dr. Kellar recommended me for it. Lots of opportunities there. Way more than here."

I will not look for the bad in this. I will be gracious and encouraging. I'm trying to save our friendship here.

"That's great, Beth. We'll miss you here." She hoped the words sounded smooth and natural, because they scratched like gravel in her throat as she forced them out.

"I know Michael had a conference call with Dr. Kellar. I think that's the first time he has talked to him. It's a shame it had to be about . . . the mess here. I hope Michael's OK. I hope he knows I had to do what was best."

The waitress arrived with their drinks, and Beth busied herself arranging the cups on the table and stirring sugar into her coffee.

Apparently Michael hadn't told Beth the details of the call with Dr. Kellar. Mia watched Beth stir. "He's fine," she said.

That was Michael. Forgiveness is paying the price for someone else. Michael didn't need Beth to know how the conference call went. And if Mia told her, the motive was only to say, "I told you so." No, she would forgive too. Sometimes forgiveness is silently paying the price.

"I leave in just two weeks," Beth said. She took a sip of her coffee. "Mmmm, I'm going to miss this."

"Well, I'm going to miss you, Beth." When Mia said the words, she meant them. But she wasn't speaking about Beth's move, she was speaking about the friendship she'd already lost.

⁕

Tea with Beth had been tougher than Mia imagined, and still there was no resolution, no magical restoration of their friendship. But Mia found that she no longer needed to justify herself to Beth or try to win a debate over the ethics of sharing Jesus. In that sense, she felt peace.

There was one more thing Mia needed to do. The picture of the door compelled her. If she could forgive Beth, then she could forgive Lily the beggar girl. And paying the price for Lily meant being willing to talk to her again. Even if she was annoying.

Mia found it difficult to ignore the nagging hopelessness she felt as she drove toward the fruit stands.

If my visit with Beth didn't fix anything, why do I think going back to Lily is going to change anything?

Mia said out loud, "Because that's not why I'm doing it. I'm not doing it to change anything. I'm doing it because it's the right thing to do."

She parked her car on the side of the road, just far enough away from the fruit stands that the men couldn't yell at her. She grabbed the little bag of food that she'd gathered to give to Lily. The little plastic bag held a bottle of water, an orange, a package of instant noodles, and a packet of cookies. Surely Lily wouldn't refuse it. She spied a group of street kids hanging out a few yards away from her under a tree.

She couldn't be sure, but she thought that she saw Lily sleeping between two of the older kids. How could they sleep on the hard ground in the middle of the day? She knew the answer, of course. This was the only kind of place they ever did sleep. But the middle of the day? Maybe she was high from sniffing paint thinner.

Mia stood beside the car. She was scared to walk over to the group of kids. Just as she turned to get back into the car, she spotted one of the boys walking toward her. His hand was out.

"*Fuloos. Fuloos,*" he said.

Oh, man, she didn't want a repeat of last time.

"No *fuloos,*" she said, shaking her head. She held out the plastic bag. Her heart pounded in her chest. As the boy approached her, she realized he was older than she'd initially thought. He was bigger too. She was standing on the side of a public road, but since she'd parked so far from the fruit stands, no one was around to see her. This boy could do whatever he wanted. She maintained her position, holding out the bag. "No *fuloos.*"

The boy stopped right in front of Mia and stared at her. He stuck a rag to his mouth and bit it. Mia smelled paint thinner, and her stomach churned. The boy looked at the bag in Mia's hand. It rattled a little, since Mia's hand was shaking.

Then he took the bag and lowered the sniffing rag. Mia saw a smile on his face. He turned and walked back to the group of kids. The bag swung at his side.

Mia got into her car and drove away.

"Thanks for drilling the hole so I can hang this picture."

"Sure, it's not like drywall back home. These cement walls are like solid rock." Michael wound up the drill cord and returned it to its box. Mia hung the framed picture over the couch and then backed up to admire it.

"There. Perfect. It's perfect."

Michael stood beside her. "Yep, looks great right there. Good idea."

Mia studied the colors and curves as if it were a famous painting hanging in an art museum. "It's like us."

"What do you mean?"

"It's rough and it's smooth. It's dark and it's light. It's a school child's colored pencils, and yet it's a masterpiece. It's us. Here in Sudan. We hate it and love it. We are scared of it and drawn to it. We bear scars and hold treasures. There is an open door, and there is much opposition. What draws it all together is God's sovereignty."

Michael grabbed Mia's hand. "And that's where we'll place our trust. Always."

A peaceful warmth ran up Mia's arm and straight into her heart. She loved this man. "Always," she replied.

Michael stared at the new piece of art. "I still don't see how you get all of that from the picture."

"Michael." Mia couldn't help laughing. "How can you not see it?"

"I don't know, babe. But there is something I do know." Michael turned Mia around to face him and he held her in his strong arms.

"Oh, yeah? What's that?"

"I signed the contract this morning. God has given us two more years in Sudan. And I have a babysitter lined up for this evening. May I have the honor of taking you out . . . finally . . . for a romantic dinner to celebrate?"

Mia smiled and laid her head on his shoulder. "Yes, you may."

Also from
Jana Kelley

In the dusty, Islamic country of Sudan, Mia's life collides with that of another young woman. A young Christian American mother, Mia finds more than one dark secret on the streets of Khartoum. She finds Halimah, a young, upper-class Arab student with a bright future in her family's business whose risky and secretive decision has put her life in danger. What happens when the path of a young mother intersects with that of a spunky Sudanese student? God transforms them both . . . forever.

If you enjoyed *Door to Freedom*, you're sure to enjoy this powerful read!

N154109
978-1-59669-430-9
$15.99

NEW HOPE®
PUBLISHERS
Gospel-Centered. Missions-Driven.

For more information, including where to purchase, please visit NewHopePublishers.com.

New Hope® Publishers is a division of WMU®, an international organization that challenges Christian believers to understand and be radically involved in God's mission. For more information about WMU, go to wmu.com. More information about New Hope books may be found at NewHopePublishers.com. New Hope books may be purchased at your local bookstore.

Use the QR reader on your
smartphone to visit us online at
NewHopePublishers.com.

If you've been blessed by this book, we would like to hear your story. The publisher and author welcome your comments and suggestions at:
newhopereader@wmu.org.